ALSO BY HAN HAN

SIMON & SCHUSTER

New York London Toronto Sydney New Delhi

THE PROBLEM WITH ME

And Other Essays
About Making Trouble
in China Today

HAN HAN

Edited and Translated
by Alice Xin Liu and
Joel Martinsen

Simon & Schuster
1230 Avenue of the Americas
New York, NY 10020

First Simon & Schuster hardcover edition August 2016

SIMON & SCHUSTER and colophon are registered trademarks
of Simon & Schuster, Inc.

For information about special discounts for bulk purchases,
please contact Simon & Schuster Special Sales at 1-866-506-1949
or business@simonandschuster.com.

The Simon & Schuster Speakers Bureau can bring authors to
your live event. For more information or to book an event,
contact the Simon & Schuster Speakers Bureau at 1-866-248-3049
or visit our website at www.simonspeakers.com.

Interior design by Lewelin Polanco

Manufactured in the United States of America

10 9 8 7 6 5 4 3 2 1

Library of Congress Cataloging-in-Publication Data

    Names: Han, Han, 1982- author. | Liu, Alice Xin, editor translator. |
Martinsen, Joel, editor, translator.
    Title: The problem with me : and other essays about making trouble in
China today / Han Han ; edited and translated by Alice Xin Liu and Joel
Martinsen.
    Description: New York : Simon & Schuster, 2016. | Includes bibli-
ographical references and index.
Identifiers: LCCN 2015030552|
    Subjects: | BISAC: POLITICAL SCIENCE / Essays. | HUMOR /
Form / Essays. | BIOGRAPHY & AUTOBIOGRAPHY / Personal
Memoirs. | HISTORY / Asia / China.
    Classification: LCC PL2939.A43 A2 2016 | DDC 895.14/52—dc23 LC
record available at http://lccn.loc.gov/2015030552

ISBN 978-1-4516-6003-6
ISBN 978-1-4516-6005-0 (ebook)

CONTENTS

TRANSLATORS' INTRODUCTION

Like no one else in China today, Han Han speaks for a new generation of troublemakers and dissidents, young people unhappy with the status quo. He first came to public attention in 1999 at the age of seventeen by winning the prestigious New Concept Writing Competition, only to soon be held back a grade, sparking a nationwide debate over how the education system could have failed someone so clearly intelligent. His semiautobiographical novel, *Triple Door*, based on his middle school experiences, was published the following year, shortly after he dropped out of high school. This propelled him to stardom and gained him a reputation as a rebel, which he lived up to, penning essays attacking education, standardized testing, and bureaucracy.

When he left school, he entered the world of car racing, going from literary prodigy to racing rookie. His persistence not only won him titles on the track but also helped with the crystallization of a philosophy: Naysayers be damned, success comes when you stick to one course of action. He filled his essays with racing, and with the people he encountered in cities and towns as he competed across the country. It was during this period, in 2005, that he launched his blog. Three years later he was China's top blogger, an influential opinion leader who lambasted corrupt officials, stood up for downtrodden citizens, and joked with porn stars with insight and wit. In his spare time, he recorded an album and launched a literary magazine.

As an Internet celebrity, Han Han found his every political thought amplified, shared and liked and debated by the celebrity-consuming public. But by 2012 a backlash against Citizen Han Han, public crusader against wrongdoing, had erupted, spawning a huge Internet debate over whether he had even authored his books. Han Han traded barbs with his attackers before bowing out. He shifted gears and turned to directing his first feature film, *The Continent*, a classic road trip movie exploring themes of loyalty, identity, and dreaming that opened in July 2014 to massive box office success and a typically divided reception. Now thirty-four, Han Han is married and the father of two children. He still polarizes opinion when he speaks of where China is headed, a concern now more personal for him than ever, because when he looks to the future, he sees his family in the rearview mirror.

This is Han Han's second book of essays to appear in English, after *This Generation: Dispatches from China's Most Popular Literary Star (and Race Car Driver)*, published in 2012 and translated and edited by Allan H. Barr. That collection contained his essays on current affairs written during a prolific two-year period at the height of his blog. However, growing up in the public eye, Han Han has left an impressive paper trail (or e-trail) through much of his life, producing a record of how China has changed over the last decade and a half and a picture of how a young person of sixteen turned into a confident man in his thirties. The essays and interviews included in this volume are drawn from a twelve-year span and evince the learning process that accompanied his transition from precocious student to influential public figure.

The present volume is not a sequel to *This Generation*. Han Han scaled back his writing activity in 2013 and now barely blogs at all, so fewer than half of the pieces here were written later than those in the earlier book. The essays here are divided thematically by the various periods of his life: student, race car driver, literary loudmouth, public intellectual, husband, and father . . . But no matter his age, Han Han has always been a troublemaker, whether a brash teenager challenging the establishment or an established public intellectual censuring those who agitate too recklessly for change. We've arranged the essays roughly chronologically, although you're welcome to begin with whichever period is of most interest to you. Footnotes have been used sparingly to explain certain in-text references, and brief introductions have been provided when we felt additional background on particular events was needed. Some of the material in this collection has been abridged.

We first began reading Han Han midway through his career, around the time he started blogging, and have been avid readers ever since, laughing at his jokes and smiling wryly at his unique take on China's often confusing contemporary life. Central to enjoying Han Han's writing is his sense of humor. But this has also made his work hard to translate. Slapstick is mixed with twists on classical quotations, and dirty jokes come alongside dry satire. The wordplay and deadpan irony Han Han deploys often requires extra cultural context, otherwise the reader might mistake him for supporting, rather than mocking, the status quo. His thoughts are humorous, pithy, and original in Chinese; this new English translation, we hope, captures that same spirit.

FOREWORD: GROWING UP IS A LONG JOURNEY
June 16, 2012

> *This essay is an abridgment of "An Eighteenth Birthday Present: A Long Journey."*

My long journey began when I was eighteen, on a train from Shanghai to Beijing.

I was unbelievably excited, because at last I was leaving my parents, my hometown, the familiar environment I'd grown up in. I was going to Beijing to leave all that behind. Even though I had no plan, I'd heard that you had to be in Beijing to work in the arts. This isn't true, let me just tell you now. Don't let the saying confuse you. You can work in the arts anywhere, as long as you have the heart.

Once on the train, I started to reminisce.

The train left in the evening, and it got dark soon after. Out the window I saw dim lights and bicycles, and I thought about myself as a boy.

I loved riding bikes. I was the Fastest Male in Tinglin. Crowds scattered before me. But I was really insecure about one thing, something that shows you how important it is to have economic independence: I rode a woman's bicycle.

Eventually, I convinced my father to buy me a mountain bike. I started going longer distances, entering the town's nooks and crannies. Like all such bikes, it was stolen in less than a year.

Let's get back on the train. In the past, no matter where I was, I was always close to home. I was never more than twelve kilometers away from home, and I'd always return at night. No matter how rebellious I was, I'd always go home.

In Beijing, I'd be more than 1,200 kilometers away. This would be my lowest period. My school experiences were all used up, and I could no longer write "campus" novels. I wanted to write novels about society. But I'd only just set foot in it myself, and it had just opened itself up to me. I would only find something I loved later: racing.

I put all my royalty payments into racing. To enter the national championships, I'd bought a car and had it modified. The car was crappy, though, since I wasn't well paid at the time. I'd see big-team racers step on the gas pedal, hear their exhaust pipes go *boom*: It was very loud. When I stepped on the gas, my exhaust pipe also went *boom*, except it was the sound of the pipe falling off.

Even though my rankings were always very poor, I was happy because I'd found a goal. I remained very happy even though I'd spent all my money and was one step away from renting an apartment in the wilderness.

Right: What I have to say has very little to do with long journeys.

I want to say your destination and the scenery along the way don't matter. But who you're with is very important: If you travel with a pig, you live in a pigsty. If a dog bites you, you have to go to the hospital.

Finding out what you love is more important than traveling. Growing up is a long journey that leaves childhood and adolescence further and further behind. During this incredibly lonely, isolating time, you will discover that the world isn't at all how you imagined, and vacationing or traveling won't

make it go away. The way I solve these problem⸍
for things I love. I like riding bikes. I like long journeys
to write. I like racing. When I was a kid I liked to read, fish for
lobsters, and play soccer. Those were my interests, life goals,
and skills. Because of this, I'm not a burden on society.

Where you go isn't important; finding what you love is.
Don't ever give up or be afraid of being laughed at. A bunch
of people will follow you around laughing at you. People will
laugh at you whether you do well or not. Even if you intend
on being the first Chinese president of the United States,
don't worry about it, just do it.

GROWING UP

Han Han was born in 1982 to middle-class parents in Tinglin, a county not far from Shanghai. His father, Han Renjun, a published writer and the director of the county's culture office, had a large influence on Han Han's reading habits. His mother, Zhou Qiaorong, worked at the local welfare office. His upbringing was a strict one, but his time outside the home was relatively unfettered: playing a lot of soccer and hanging out with his school chums. He was admitted to a selective middle school on the basis of athletic performance, but was a lackluster student. Writing was his creative outlet, and by 2000—the year he dropped out of school—he had won multiple essay contests and was finishing his first novel, *Triple Door*. That semiautobiographical story of an unmotivated student filtered his own experiences through the styles of two of his literary heroes, the 1940s satirist Qian Zhongshu and the 1990s "hooligan" writer Wang Shuo. The book sold 20 million copies, and Han Han became a national celebrity and an antiestablishment hero.

I GREW UP WITH BLUE SKIES
First published in 2000

I call my childhood the era of blue skies because, from what I can remember, it almost never rained, and above me were white clouds and blue skies. Childhood in today's cities can only be called "gray." Children are forced to practice piano from the age of five till fifteen. If they pass a level each year, then in ten years they'll pass ten. A few days ago I went to listen to a boy who had practiced piano from a young age, and I realized that in the human world it's not terrible to play the zither to an ox; it's worse to have the ox play the zither to you. It's fine to stand there and listen to it for four or five seconds, but it's hard work and perseverance to listen to it for twelve. Many good-hearted parents offer this explanation: "Practice when you're young, and it'll be good for you when you're old." As for not being able to have fun as a child: "Wait till you have a successful career, and fame and fortune, and then you can make up for it." But how can they be so idiotic that they don't realize that childhood play is the purest form of play, and that when they become rich and famous, play is basically mah-jongg and cards? Are these interchangeable? Even if they are, when you retire, are you going to meet up with a bunch of other retirees to play marbles, fish for lobsters, or watch *Calabash Brothers*? You'll never get back what you've lost. Don't think that it's as easy to make up for regrets as it is for the goddess Nüwa to mend the sky.

I grew up in a village in the countryside. The countryside really is a good place, for at the very least you can sing as loudly as you like, not like in the cities. If you want to sing loudly there, unless you sing really well, you'll very soon collect all kinds of strange people. My next door neighbor Xiaofeng was dubbed "Singing King" when he was a kid, since he apparently wrote songs and lyrics and performed them from the age of four. Later he gave up his entertainment career to become a fashion model. No matter what the garment, he'd put it on. He could even wear a suit jacket with shorts and galoshes. This was the outfit he wore in junior high. What a shame that at the time no one considered him a role model for breaking through feudalism. He certainly didn't lack vision. It was around this time that conscientiousness over name brands began, although the shame of it was that people had such slim wallets, they had to go to street stalls, where Nike sneakers were 10 yuan. You could feel your social status shoot up after you put on a pair, so who cared if they were fakes or not. And we would ignore the Nike swoosh that went in the wrong direction, or had a smaller swoosh emerging from the middle of the big one. Xiaofeng didn't really seem to have a concept of this. At that time, I was in junior high in the county seat and would come back once every couple of weeks. The first thing I'd do after arriving was go to see what outfit he was showing off that day. Later, his clothes became more and more standard, no different from what the kids on the street were wearing, and I grew disappointed.

Xiaofeng is now a student at a vocational school, and in his words he is unable to study. In reality, the kid's pretty smart, but fortune wasn't fair. Terrible people get better at their studies, but if Xiaofeng studied to get better, he'd only get worse. Still, every time Xiaofeng sees me, he praises the vocational school up to the heavens, talking about it so much that I've started to itch for heaven myself. The kid is studying environmental protection right now, and often goes on about its importance. When he gets excited, he moistens his lips and spits on the floor and says, "Of course, that's how it is theoretically. But it doesn't work out like that in practice."

As for playing basketball, Xiaofeng was a real top player. He was a couple notches behind me on the soccer field, so he had to practice basketball really hard. There was a backboard in my rural elementary school, set a couple of centimeters lower than what was standard because it was a child's backboard. Xiaofeng would hang on to the basket, totally wrecking it. And so he became a public enemy of the Party, the people, and every basketball lover. Later he changed his ways and stopped hanging on to the basket, and focused instead on his shooting. Because he was used to playing on this court, as soon as he played on a real court he didn't know how to use all the strength he had. So all those self-imposed hardships eventually kept his body strong and healthy and greatly improved his basketball skills.

Xiaofeng had a brother, a student at Tongji University, who was three years older. He also used to go to vocational school, but later he "righted a wrong" and entered university under the auspices of the vocational-technical-professional program. There's a saying that goes, "Play at Fudan, eat at Tongji, love at South China Normal, live at Jiao Tong," and sure enough that was the case: When I saw the guy again after he'd been there a year, he was a fat cat and declared that going to Tongji hadn't been a waste. And the kid started to soar intellectually; he started to think that his name, Chunfeng, sounded boring. When we were young, we'd often make fun of the meaning of his name, "spring winds," using the song

"Little Grass": "Spring winds, oh, spring winds, you've blown me till I'm green." Chunfeng thought that we kids were immature and he was extremely dismissive of my essays. He said he'd be embarrassed to wipe his ass with them: He'd be embarrassed for his ass.

Chunfeng was a good student and studied hard at university. He didn't touch alcohol or cigarettes, and he didn't have a girlfriend. Last year good news came, news that astounded the village. He'd been awarded a scholarship worth 3,000 yuan. And so the entire population saw him as their model, and should have made a statue of him to erect at the front of the village.

Xiaofeng and Chunfeng's father was the village chief, a figure of authority. He didn't usually beat his sons to educate them, since he couldn't bear to, but when he was unable to stand it any longer he'd get whichever one he could find and then the village would resound with his beatings.

Educated by the village chief, the two sons didn't have any bad habits. I'll have you know that it's extremely rare to have sons as well trained as these in a village, and so the village head had even more authority than before. When the villagers had problems—big problems like the murder of a mother, and small problems like the theft of an old hen—they would go talk to him.

Out of the guys who played together as children, there was also a large and bulky guy called Chunping. This year he's entering the second year of junior high but still hasn't started puberty. He looks the same as he did three years ago. Chunping was talented and had a clean look. Adults predicted three years ago that he'd grow up to take China by storm, not realizing that after three years had passed he wouldn't have grown up at all, so they had no choice but to postpone their predictions.

Out of everyone in the village, Chunping's grandmother adored children the most. But unfortunately she was blind, and while in theory she would have kept one eye open and one eye closed when it came to educating Chunping, this didn't play out in reality. She was old, and couldn't walk far, and so she used the "thousand-*li* yell" technique. She'd step out of the house and roar "Chun—Ping!" and you'd think she was going to cut someone to pieces. But after Chunping got home, she'd grip her grandson and wouldn't stop caressing him. Our worries were all for nothing.

Our view was that, once Chunping grew up, he would no longer be cute. People cuddle puppies because they're little, but no one's ever seen a pretty maiden holding a meter-long wolfhound in her lap.

Chunping's neighbor was as old as he was, but he'd already started puberty, and his voice had broken. Chunping's parents especially admired this, and they'd often ask his parents what their secret was. The two kids were more or less taking their first steps into adolescence together, and they already knew how to show off. They learned basketball from Xiaofeng, and both of them became Lords of Traveling. The explanation Chunfeng gave for this was: "At such a young age, taking a few steps is fine. The referee won't blow his whistle."

And another noteworthy figure is Wei Di. He's only three days younger than me, but my image of myself as the mature one is based on those three days. If a small difference made him three days older than me, then he'd be my older brother and I'd have to call him Wei Ge, as in "Viagra." The houses in our village all stood parallel to each other; only Wei Di's house exhibited a kind of independent thinking, towering all alone at the front and "monopolizing the dragon's pulse," in feng shui terms. Its location was uniquely blessed: It was surrounded on three sides by fields, and at the back a small river meandered. A fierce-looking dog was chained in the woods. Imagine martial artists flitting here and there among the trees, when suddenly a martial hound would appear. Pair it with some superstar, and it has something of the spirit of how the eagle shows up behind Yang Guo in *The Return of the Condor Heroes*. It's just a shame that the dog lacked vigor. This dog collected in itself the spirit of both sky and earth: It had a hypersensitive sense of smell. As soon as someone came within a radius of five hundred meters he would bark non-stop, and even stranger, as soon as the same person entered a five-meter radius, the dog would show incredible obedience and lie on the ground moaning. We painstakingly designed a security plan. It wasn't enough to wage war on the ground; we also considered using an airdrop. Except who could know whether the dog would smell you five hundred meters above in the sky. Because the dog's sense of smell was too sensitive, it was never quiet near Wei Di's house. Yet Wei Di was well-known as a good student for the new century, and he had big ambitions to help build the Four Modernizations. The sound of the winds, the rain, or the dog didn't bother him.

For an important exam, Wei Di's test scores would be un-usually stable. Usually everyone would know what his scores would be before he took the exam. Wei Di didn't do so well in his junior high exams two years ago, making just 471.5, but that was what was needed to enter the best high school in the district that year, so no points were wasted. When I was still a child, Wei Di was much better known for reading than I was because I read only unofficial books. In the villages, unofficial books can never enter the halls of hallowed literature, but Wei Di read the correct books, murmuring every day: "If the one's place is too small, borrow from the tens'. If the tens' place is too small, borrow from the hundreds'." With all the borrowing, people thought Wei Di owed somebody a lot of money. You could see Wei Di's passion for reading when he played chess: He'd hide a book in his jacket, which he read whenever he had the chance.

He went to the district senior high, and the school wasn't far from me, so I went to visit him but couldn't find him for ages. I'd find him later curled up in the corner doing test questions.

These are all the characters from the era of the blue skies. I don't want to talk about their childhoods but about who they became as adults, because I can see their childhoods based on what they're like now. I don't want to share happiness; I still think, selfishly, that happiness and pain can't be shared. In the end, you have to digest these things yourself. I wrote this down so people would know. Now the brothers have scattered to every corner of Shanghai, and in the future they will scatter all over China. I'm infringing on their reputations by writing this down as a commemoration. Commemoration finished.

SOCCER, AH, SOCCER
First published in 2000

In elementary school we didn't know the game was called soccer. We called it "leatherball," and we played the rugby way. People over the age of sixty today basically have no concept of soccer. Every time I'm home and I kick a ball around with friends, some old woman off to the side will mumble "Slapping the leatherball, Han Han?" through her toothless mouth. My enthusiasm plummets whenever I hear her say this. You might assume that slapping a leatherball wouldn't be a big deal, what with the state of our national team, but for kids like us who were fanatical about soccer, it was a different matter.

I got into soccer in the first year of middle school. Our school was enormous back then; I was in Class 14, a number big enough to make you spit out your food. The first-year syllabus was pretty lax, and we'd play soccer every evening after school let out. My skills were lacking back then, and I was always the substitute. Being dissatisfied, I trained hard every day. Every weekend that year I would go home and practice on an abandoned cement floor, perfect for a novice like me who'd smack the ball twenty meters as soon as I touched it. I would set out some Coke bottles on the ground and practice dribbling. Since there was no one to pass to, I had to dribble alone, which gave me the bad habit of dribbling too much later on. There used to be a little black dog tied up near my house, and the door to the doghouse turned out to be just the size I wanted.

Even though I loved the dog as much as my life, I threw all that aside for the sake of self-improvement and chose to sacrifice the dog to my cause. My footwork was terrible at first, so the dog was relatively safe, and had no sense of anything but a *whoosh* going past its house. But one day a hard kick sent the ball inside. The poor dog, unaware of my superhumanly fast progress, was totally unprepared for the day I would score; all it could do was jump with a heartrending yelp. After that, my ball kicking continued to improve, so the dog was forced to remain homeless. The progress I made in ball kicking was due, in no small part, to the dog's selfless assistance, but regrettably it passed on after ingesting poisoned dog food. Five years later, the dog may be gone, but I often think about how I used to practice shots in the weak orange lamplight.

Because my skills increased so quickly, by the time I was a second-year student, I was one of the more distinguished players in Class 14. Whenever school let out, we'd take a leather soccer ball to the basketball court and play till sunset. To this day I still remember some of the more peculiar people in the class, and years on I still have a laugh with my old friends.

One of them was our class leader, Yu Zongping, who's now at the high school affiliated with Fudan University. His skills were fairly well-rounded, and he was distinguished by his big head, the better to handle all kinds of information. The guy played with an eerie calmness and was a skilled playmaker. Since his head was so big, he made for a large target, and on late crosses we'd aim right for it. He was so poor at getting around opponents that every time he had to, there would be a lengthy battle. This inevitably resulted in feet getting kicked, and when that happened, the entire school would hear it. When he dribbled, we really understood how cruel soccer could be.

Another was Zhang Xiaofeng, who's at the Jinshan District

high school now. He's got the same name as an old Taiwanese writer, but outclasses her only where speed is concerned. Zhang Xiaofeng made his name by speed, and could do a hundred meters in eleven seconds. Speed isn't always a good thing, though. For example, Zhang Xiaofeng's biggest problem was that he'd always run faster than the ball. You'd see him zip out from the pack like a thunderbolt, and head for the keeper like a knife. But as the crowd remained astonished, Zhang and the keeper would be looking at each other with helplessness, and then everyone would realize at the same time that the ball was still back in the pack. Zhang Xiaofeng was also pretty strong; he practically could have used a few of the thinner team members as toothpicks. What distinguished him from Yu Zongping was that he made contact with his body rather than his feet, and five meters from a person he'd usually stop kicking and simply barrel down on them. Like the style of certain athletes, if he could slam them aside, it didn't matter if he could outkick them. That's the tragedy of soccer: When the players can't tell whether they're kicking a ball or playing snooker.

Another legendary individual was Shi Xiaobo. This guy never used his feet. It was all hands. He was a born defender, with a great Iron Palm that never failed him when he was defending: No matter how good your ball skills were, you couldn't escape getting hit. A few days ago, when my Chinese teacher got to Mencius's line about food, "Bear paw is also what I desire," my first reaction was to think of Shi Xiaobo. The place he guarded was known as the Bermuda Triangle, and people with poor self-defense saw it as a treacherous mountain pass that they had to detour around rather than go through. Another reason to remember him was his unusually powerful shot. As the defender, he rarely made shots on goal, but when he had the chance, he'd boot it as hard as he could.

Yet, compared to my achievements shooting at the doghouse, his precision was poor. With my special training, I'd get energized whenever I took a shot because the goal would turn into a doghouse. But Shi Xiaobo didn't have that advantage. People in the line of his shot typically had two possible fates: They turned into motionless, standing "vegetables"; or they went down on all fours like "animals." In one game, Zhang Xiaofeng, strong as an ox, ended up as an animal after a smack from Shi Xiaobo, so you get the idea.

Last is Xu Ming, who's now at the high school affiliated with Jiao Tong University. He was a typical theorist. He consumed the classics, from records of soccer clubs down to the substitute defender's girlfriend's mother's occupation; he knew it all like the back of his hand. Tall and well-built, Xu Ming was perfect for soccer, except for his 20/700–800 vision. When he took off his glasses he turned into a blind man feeling an elephant, with no hope of shooting at the goal. Apart from directing from the sidelines, Xu Ming would sometimes take to the field to practice a few kicks; but when the ball rolled slowly toward him, his kick would land on air, a false alarm. All of us had suffered his abuse. And when Xu Ming cursed at you, he'd leave himself out of the equation entirely, point at your nose, and lay into you for not knowing how to play soccer. He was adept at the 3-3-4, 3-4-3, and 2-5-3 formations, and he knew when to switch them up. Once, he even set out a 3-5-3 formation, and we puzzled over where the extra man came from until he explained that the keeper would, on his own initiative, become mobile by charging from the penalty area into midfield if he wasn't satisfied with guarding the goal. And so the keeper would lurk for long stretches in the penalty area, and a Luoxing Middle School soccer spectacle was born.

The class went through some tremendous ups and downs

during our second-year all-school tournament, but we ultimately snatched the title. That day the whole team was beaming and we bid a temporary farewell to the field. We seldom played a real game after third year started.

The summer after our high school entrance exams was the World Cup. I didn't want the Chinese team to make the competition because that would mean standards had fallen. It would be a waste of ink for me to rate the national men's team in this essay. The 1998 World Cup wasn't all that spectacular, but Michael Owen's goal gave us a vague glimpse of Zhang Xiaofeng's style.

My old twilight soccer friends from Luoxing Middle School have all gone their separate ways. I've only been in touch very infrequently by phone, and we've never gotten together to play a game. When the clock in the old school's clock tower strikes five, there's no one left to say, "That's it, stop playing," and at five thirty a group of unfamiliar kids, instead of us, will go to the shop and buy orange soda for fifty cents. They look unfamiliar, but they also look like the same old soccer chums.

In high school, I often played soccer on the weekends. I should say that my high school classmates were pretty good. Wencius, a guy with a passion for literature, was better than average. I'd argue with him endlessly about who was better. But impressiveness doesn't just come with being better. Like Xiao Lu in the next dorm room over, the focus of attention because of his enormous kicks. If there was a ball at his feet, he'd boot it. There's really nothing special about enormous kicks, and as defender, you've got to do them. But Xiao Lu held people's attention because his enormous kicks always headed toward his own team's goal. Even though we played for years together, Wenzi and I couldn't understand how Xiao Lu, with his back turned, would shoot at his own goal. In the

1999 tournament, we didn't even make it out of group. I must admit that I played pretty badly. I just didn't feel anything when I played with those teammates.

The last thing I'll talk about is the Xinmin Evening News Cup, which I played in twice. Both times were under the cruel summer sun, so after getting back from playing, it was like we'd changed nationalities. I didn't want to take part at first, but I did because we had so few venues to play in. Playing alleyway soccer wasn't bad, but halfway through a game a neighbor would pick up a weapon and go after the ball, since people in the community said it was too loud. Ordinary folk in China are like that: They can tolerate mah-jongg but can't tolerate a soccer match. So I applied for those two Xinmin Evening News Cups, since I had nowhere else to go. The worst headache about taking part was that you needed the school's seal and your homeroom teacher's permission, which raised the question of who was participating, us or our principal and teachers? Another headache was picking a team name. You wanted a name to rouse the spirit, so "Big White Bunny" or "Spotted Dogs" were definitely out, since your opponents' laughter would disrupt your game. "Shenhua" after Shanghai's club was already taken, and while "Peanuts" wasn't a bad idea, names like "Supermen" and "The Dream Team," while not embarrassing, weren't great for chanting out loud. In order not to crack you up, I'll refrain from telling you what our actual name was.

The Xinmin Evening News Cup was nothing more than a way to work up a sweat and change nationalities during the summer holiday, but some of the habits gained through those tournaments have never changed, like getting the fifty-cent bottle of soda when the Luoxing Middle School's evening bell sounds.

THOSE PEOPLE, THOSE THINGS
First published in 2000

I used to yearn for dormitory life, because I confused living in a dormitory with renting an apartment. I thought that boarding school would be incredibly liberating, but I realized after a year that there's a world of difference between the two concepts. No one can prevent you from doing what you like inside your own apartment unless someone is tearing the place down, but the dorm has all kinds of rules. I measured myself against them and discovered that, apart from possession of banned weapons, I'd violated all the rest.

I was full of curiosity when I enrolled in Shanghai's Songjiang No. 2 High School, especially after I heard that their rooms were a standard two-bedroom/one living room layout. Getting that floor plan, with a double-urinal toilet, is a happy thing in the life of a student. It was only after I enrolled that I found out they weren't joking about the two-and-one; it's just that it had to be shared by sixteen people. My dorm mates and I were together for one and a half years. We laughed, played, bickered, and fought, but I'm not sure about crying, since that's an under-the-sheets affair.

Now when I sit down to think about my friends and their typical expressions, everything comes flooding back. (I've got a new set now, and they're just as fun.) The most fun came from "Midnight Cough King," who lived not far from the dorm room. He had an exceptional habit: An hour after lights out, he would cough three times, loud enough for all of Song-jiang District to hear. This persisted for several months, never breaking for rain, louder and more punctual than a cockcrow, and a sign that the midnight music program was about to come on. His achievements will be remembered for a thousand autumns. It seems prosaic when I think about it now, but if, decades from now, I hear his cough again, it may trigger the same feelings, a souvenir of that particular time period. To remember, I need to write out character sketches, in order to get a laugh when I'm bored.

Jiecius was head of our dorm room. He was an excellent room leader and made us keep our voices low, mainly because it would affect his sleep. Like all pure and simple working folk, he woke at dawn, slept at sunset, and followed a careful routine, setting a fairly significant example for all of us.

He was the serious one in room 205 in the boys' dorm, and also the most innocent; I don't believe any romantic fantasies ever materialized for him. But Jiecius possessed the great power of communication, because he was responsible for managing the mailboxes and the telephone, only regrettably there were never any letters or phone calls for him. Living under such conditions might screw you up, so we were worried that an unbalanced Jiecius might swallow the telephone, which he fortunately never did.

President, one of the few male cadres in our class, imagined his post to be the highest, but there's always someone higher—in his case, the branch secretary of the youth league. President's real power was less than the dorm leader's, less even than the television monitor's. He had one duty: to attend various school meetings and take detailed notes so messages could be passed along. Cadres in the student association enjoyed the pleasures of their office and asked for class presidents every two or three days, since there'd be nothing for them to do otherwise.

In the second semester of 1999, we received some bad news: President's father was killed in a car crash, and in grief he departed. Bad luck also visited a Propaganda Committee member, since he had to attend meetings in President's place. We imagined that President's personality would have changed significantly upon his return, but he turned out to be unexpectedly strong-willed.

We used to like cracking jokes about him, but these dropped off sharply after his father died, and even though he didn't seem to have changed much at all, we caught a glimpse of the effect of his father's passing in the way he would inexplicably stare off into the distance when he was alone.

We had the habit of altering our mates' surnames as a sign of respect, but Fencius wasn't as refined as his nickname implied. He was an ordinary guy with rough edges, hair you could use to fly a kite, and whiskers you could use to catch fish. He stood just five feet three inches tall. When boxing became popular in our dorm in 1999, a kid next door, who gave himself the nickname "No. 1 Bodybuilder" and had biceps bigger than his head, beat Fencius around so badly, he was left looking for his teeth.

Fencius had the bunk closest to the door—a crappy position, because it was nearest to the light switch. In the second semester, Jiecius suffered from a weird recurring illness, "Lights-out Syndrome." Whenever it got to lights-out, he'd get excited as hell, praising the light and lashing out at the darkness in poems he recited nonstop. This left Fencius with the task of turning out the lights. He had short arms, meaning an excruciating near-death exposure to the elements every time he did so. On cold winter nights, he was especially reluctant to leave his covers. But we'd receive a demerit if our room lights were turned off late.

Fencius's unique talent was soccer. His style was as crude as he looked, running flat-out and often trying to scissor the ball when it was still several meters away. No one went near him when we played so as not to lose an organ. He'd take the ball out of bounds, frequently leaving the field with it even when there were no defenders. In light of this skill set, we dispatched him to play defense. When a striker from the other team saw him, they'd detour so as to live a little longer. Still, our soccer team didn't make the semifinals of the interschool league, my biggest regret of that year.

Now we move on to my deskmate Lecius, the first guy I ever had for a deskmate. He had a stubborn streak he often put into his studies, and sometimes he wouldn't go to the toilet unless he conquered a diabolically difficult question. He'd hold it in until both inspiration and pee came out. Sometimes, in order to speed up writing, he'd hold his breath, write one line, and then breathe. For a while, it felt like we had an ox in our classroom.

He evangelized this carry-on-until-there's-no-more-hope–ism, saying "In whatever you do, you have to persevere." He'd also quote the words of a famous Westerner, "Not even a cannon could change my mind if there's something I want to do." He'd often say to me, "You've got to be hard like a brick wall." But after reading recent reports on "tofu dregs"* engineering projects, he revised this: "Like a decently built brick wall."

---

* Tofu dregs, which crumble at the slightest touch, have become the go-to image for referring to building and infrastructure projects that use substandard materials and shoddy design to cut costs during construction.

Juncius was the strongest one in our dorm room. He was famous for his muscles as well as his love for soup left over from instant noodles. His muscles, carefully cultivated through hard work, were more important than life to him, and as soon as he returned to the dorm he'd be showing them off. He hated the school rules, because they stopped him from walking into the classroom in his underpants. But his muscle building had an unlikely contrast in his love for soup. At night, we had the habit of eating instant noodles in our dorm room—all kinds of noodles—and naturally, there'd be plenty of soup left neglected in the bowls. At this point we would summon Juncius, who would materialize before your noodle bowl and slurp up the soup. He'd say, "Seven parts soup has six parts nutrition. Soup is the source of life and is immensely important." No wonder he was so fit: He was being nourished by that six parts of nutrition.

Juncius didn't have the best grades. He barely passed, and so just like me it was difficult for him to enter the next grade. In the final days before our exams, Juncius and I, as well as Danyang, who also had bad grades, stayed up all night. I remember the torrential rain that night as we walked with our backs against the wall to get dumplings to fill our empty stomachs at midnight. As it turned out, the dumplings were so fragrant and delicious that we'd eaten them all before midnight came. It was hard going, staying up the whole night, and we had to take the table and chairs into the corridor to get paltry scraps of light. The dozen-watt bulb was dim and made our eyes sore, and the only comfort was the night radio program: a husky voice reverberating lazily in the darkness, adding flourishes of tragedy to the scene. We leafed through books, wrote letters, stared ahead, shot the breeze, showed off, complained, sighed, kept quiet, made tea, hit our heads and stomped our feet, showered, listened to the rain, shut the window, opened the door, took a short rest, awoke with a start, meditated, played cards, went crazy, and dreamed as the night passed, never to return. Pretty soon a bunch of idiots discovered that this life was pretty sweet, so one by one they came to stay up overnight. A few dozen people leafing through books, writing letters, staring ahead, shooting the breeze, showing off. . . . No different from what happens in a classroom. The outcome of staying up all night was negligible. Juncius realized a tragic truth: Lots of hard work may have no effect. Even so, he remained at the top of the bad students and caught a lucky break to advance to the next grade. However, although we said we would, we didn't stuff ourselves with dumplings to celebrate. Who knows whether he'll ever realize another truth: Lots of promises may have no fulfillment.

A week later, I used an entire roll of film taking pictures for the dorm room and edited them into a story, capturing my comrades' voices and smiling faces. In the photos, Fencius and Lecius have their eyes closed, Jiecius's head is obscuring Juncius's pecs (he was really upset about this, but it was too late to change, and I could only get his profile), Danyang looks so stupid he makes the viewer crack up, and Chao'an is getting shoved and looks wondrously like Superman about to take flight. The faces framed in these pictures, smiling and not, will help lock away in my memory times both happy and sad.

My new dorm room is next to the old one, and the guys I live with just keep getting more and more likable. One day someone was inspired to attach two-digit numbers to the bunks, 01, 02, and so forth, which we referred to as "Oh-One," "Oh-Two," etc. We've reached Oh-Ten—that is, 010, although Oh-Two says it should be called Oh-One-Oh. I'm in Oh-One, so it fell to me to devise an entry password to re-place the old one: "Don't ask where I'm going" was the challenge, and the reply was "My hometown is in Shaanxi," which was kind of lame. Now it's been officially changed to "You've had our wine" and "Feels so good when it cleans you out." We made a pact to share our difficulties, but enjoy our good fortune alone.

Xiao Lu lives in Oh-Two. He's fairly avant-garde, and wears a beeper that, apart from going *deet-deet-deet* at six in the morning to wake people up, regrettably doesn't do anything else. Xiao Lu is also pretty restless, and the "October Ninth Tragedy" in our dorm was the result of this tendency. He was kicking Wencius's bunk and kicked the bedboard so hard that it fell. Wencius had the good fortune not to die; the only injury he suffered was to his brain, so that for a time he was unable to differentiate between subjects, predicates, and objects. Xiao Lu got stuck underneath the bedboard, like a turtle without its feet. After a long time, he crawled out of the debris and said: "Soooo good." And thus we observed Xiao Lu's incredible ability to take a beating. It was only later that we found out that his best skill was on the phone. Unless he had an outside reason, like lights-out or a desperate need to pee, he could stay on the phone till the phone itself rotted away.

Ph.D. is from my hometown, but he is more rear-garde than Xiao Lu. He gained his nickname because he said he knew all the answers on the *Arena of Stars* educational quiz show. Later we found out this was a lie: It is quite possible that Ph.D. can't even list the seven continents and nine planets. He also can't sit still, and although he likes to tell jokes, his jokes are groan-worthy and draw laughter from no one apart from himself. As if to make up for this defect, Ph.D. is really good at blowing—I mean, playing the Chinese flute. I remember one Sunday when Ph.D. brought a bunch of different sticks from home. We thought at first that they were for drying clothes, then we guessed that he wanted to improve our diet by fishing in the high school's pond or taking down sparrows. Unexpectedly, he put a stick next to his mouth, and in alarm we worried he would swallow it and kill himself. Instead, he played a beautiful tune, and we finally realized what it was. What a shame, though, that after studying hard for two years, he could play only a tune that conjured up cows and horses grazing happily on the grassland.

Later on, Ph.D. played the flute at shows put on by various classes, to general acclaim. Everyone said he could blow like a champ.

Wencius sleeps on the bunk next to Ph.D., and I met him first. I lived in the dorm next door at the time, and my dorm mate showered praise on Wencius. Wencius, he said, was an uncommon talent in the current generation of literati, so I really wanted to meet him. I did, and he's fairly average, a bookworm with the balance tilted toward the worm side.

Forming words and sentences is clearly kids' stuff for Wencius, and he's worked hard reading books and practicing characters in order to one day rise to an adult level. Reading a book is a fine and meticulous job for him: If you give him a book in the morning and ask him how many pages he's read, his answer will be about a hundred; ask him in the afternoon, and the brilliant answer will be that he is on page ninety. "Wencius, back to front is not a good way to read," I'll say. "You don't even know what you're reading." His explanation: "The best part of a book is its bottom." Who knows where he got this from, but it is obvious he's misunderstood.

It's true that wisdom's on the bottom, but a bottom sits in the middle of a person.

For the past few days, a trendy game in our dorm has been "Jump up and touch the beam." If you can't reach it, you're no longer among the ranks of men. Wencius couldn't reach it, so he went out on to the balcony crying that he was no longer a man. Xiao Zhi is the manliest of all in our dorm. His hand went right past the beam when he jumped. If we want to talk about Xiao Zhi, we have to start with basketball. He's a point scorer and barely moves an inch when he plays; he simply stares unflinchingly down the court until a teammate passes him the ball, and then he runs forward with it. This obviously tarnishes the visual nature of basketball, and so we punish him by not allowing him in the center. Xiao Zhi has to work hard on his mid-range jump shot. His favorite phrase is "*Sooo* awkward," which he says with tonal modulation that gives it extra flavor. He's moved out of the dorm and into a new place, so in the future I'll never hear "*Sooo* awkward" again.

Xiao Qing imagines himself to be quite humorous. He thinks that if there are ten points of humor throughout the world, then he has five, and I have four, and everyone else in the world put together shares the last one. He imagines he possesses great literary talent. "Brother Han," he often says, "I have to admit I'm just a little funnier than you today." Xiao Qing really likes to sing, but he sticks to a single note, with each song distinguished only by how heavily or lightly he pronounces the words. It doesn't make a difference how high or low the note is. His favorite lyric is from one of the themes to the *Young and Dangerous* movies: "There are red stars all around."

Jiajia and Milk Candy are like their names sound: They look soft and feminine. Jiajia's specialty is that he loves to pose, and once he decides on one, a dozen people can't dissuade him from it. Lately he's fallen in love with singing by taking Xiao Qing as his master. The strange part of his singing is that no one can imitate him, even when he's out of tune. You can't even use him for jokes in the classroom. That's what it means to have a standard.

"O Pressed Salted Duck" rises the earliest out of everyone in the dorm. His nickname comes from the time he brought us a pressed salted duck when he came back from Nanjing. It was absolutely delicious and the memory has never faded, so we're reminded of it every time we see him. As for the "O," that came from the fact that he went to Australia once and had to transfer through Osaka, which sounds like "pressed salted duck" when the characters are read in Chinese, and so we put the two together. He's a generous person, and he never eats all the duck feed, but saves it for the hardworking masses.

Yesterday was my last night in the dorm. People should leave on a good note, and so my mates and I talked half the night away. I'll be moving to room 101, just beneath them, and each night before going to sleep I'll remind my previous dorm mates to stomp three times in order to say good-bye.

THE PROBLEM WITH TEACHERS
2003

The Chinese education system is terrible because the teachers are terrible.

Children easily idolize people who seem knowledgeable, and in a class of young virgin boys a teacher is, at the very least, an adult in their eyes, therefore even a pervert will gain the class's deepest respect. We really scrape the barrel with elementary school teachers. Teachers are generally trained at low-end schools. Only those with bad grades, no special talent, no desire to be a soldier, and no desire to be associated with vocational school would choose to attend teachers college. If they learned something at teachers college, if they were good-looking, or if they had superb grades, they would not have chosen the teaching profession. So those who end up staying at teachers colleges are the poor-scoring, untalented ones uninterested in the army and who hate the way *unemployed* sounds to other people. Just imagine how capable they are.

China has tried to elevate the status of teachers for thousands of years, and their status today is inappropriate. Teaching has been called the most glorious occupation under the sun. If we're being honest, teaching is just one of many jobs, and a way to support your family. It's not fundamentally different from driving a taxi or cleaning a house. If teachers all around the world were paid only 200 yuan a month, then perhaps it really could be called the most glorious and self-sacrificing occupation under the sun. The thing to remember is that teaching is an extremely simple, cyclical job, and so long as the textbooks are the same, the same things are said every two or three years, over and over. They'll even use the same old lame jokes to lighten the mood. If you get held back and you happen to have the same teacher, you'll recognize this. Even test papers can be reused, as long as the brats from the previous year hold their tongues. Math, physics, chemistry, English, history, and geography test papers can be reused your entire life. Apart from ticking boxes, there is no other physical effort required. Standing while teaching lessons isn't even hard, just as sitting down isn't a luxury for taxi drivers. The key reason for teaching being credited as the most glorious occupation under the sun is that, apart from going to the canteen for food, teachers rarely appear in sunlight.

When I was at school, their worst tactic was saying, "I want to see your parents." What an utterly comical statement. First of all, they can't even educate a minor, let alone an adult. Also, I think if a student does something wrong, the school or the teacher holds greater responsibility than the parents or the students. In the event of something serious, a phone call will suffice; but there's no need for parents to ask for time off so they can go in themselves. It's over-the-top. Some parents have to ask for leave and ride a couple hours on a bus, thinking the entire time that their kid must have committed murder, when it's really nothing more than an incorrectly hung towel and a deduction of dorm points. If I were the parent, I'd beat up the teacher who called me in. No, actually I couldn't do that. First of all, my kid has his reputation to protect, and secondly, if I went to town, I'd be outnumbered by teachers. But you've got to vent your anger somewhere, so you end up beating your kid. And, so in a way, the goal of calling you in has been achieved.

Just now, I touched on deducting points for conduct that violates some rule. There's no such thing as standard conduct. Sometimes people need order, but when something normal is measured by grades and rankings, it turns abnormal, because now there's a direct relationship to a teacher's bonuses and reputation, and then we're back to "I need to see your parents."

One of the biggest mistakes teachers and schools tend to make is to isolate those they're not fond of. For example, a teacher may influence the other students to despise a student who is always failing and pulling down the class average, or punish the whole class for his mistake, as well as doing other things that demean the teaching profession. These teachers aim to exclude poorly performing students from those who still have undeveloped psychologies. There would be no point in doing any of this if that wasn't the goal.

During the SARS outbreak, some airlines launched a 40 percent discount for teachers and medical staff. People were highly skeptical: So female teachers were being sent to the front line because there weren't enough nurses? I really couldn't see what teachers had to do with SARS aside from teaching people to wash their hands. So the logic follows: If I worked in sanitation, could I get 40 percent off my airfare?

Seriously, though, teaching really is a very respectable profession, if you don't mind that there's no future in it and that no matter how much you try, you'll always just be a teacher.

THE PROBLEM WITH CADRES
2003

I can't believe I was on the student committee in elementary school. I think back to it today and it seems like a miracle that this happened. And the miracle within a miracle was that I was class monitor for mathematics.

I may have been class monitor, but a "class cadre"? Forget it. Elementary and high school students are still innocent, so why subject them to such filth so early?

Cadres. Everywhere you look in China there are cadres, even in the classrooms. Out of just forty people in a class, ten are cadres, but that does reflect society as we know it. Children start getting perverted from a young age, and their parents get perverted along with them. Being class vice president is enough to make the parents ecstatic. Bribes don't even come into it yet.

The class cadre system is a pedantic part of the Chinese education system, and it doesn't help the students with their organizational skills. Those with real organizational skills are already adept at organizing secret criminal activity, but all the class cadres—or teacher's pets—have learned from their good grades is how to abuse power.

One problem for Chinese people, particularly officials, is that the lower they are in status, the more they abuse their power. A hotel security guard or a parking lot attendant must think they're shitting priceless gold nuggets.

It's the same with class cadres. There is a class monitor

for study, a class monitor for work, a league secretary, a class president, a class vice president, a class monitor for sports, a class monitor for the arts, so on and so forth. Why do we need so many class cadres? The Chinese government has far too many agencies and a much too complicated staff. Basically, there are too few people doing real work, and too many good-for-nothings.

But good-for-nothings are fine unless they're degenerates.

That goes for class organizations, too. Class cadres don't do anything, but they know how to instruct others, and for that purpose they're told to wear one stripe, two stripes, or three stripes pinned to their sleeves to show their rank and the difference between them and the "ordinary folk."

I think, aside from military rank, we need to get rid of systems such as these. It's only a matter of time until Chinese officials begin to draw stars on their foreheads to mark themselves out. Yet status distinctions begin in elementary school, and this is the norm for most people. When parents and kids are out on a Sunday, the kids are still wearing their stripes from school. If one bumps into another with three stripes, the first will think the second's the shit. A kid with two stripes who sees one who has three will think, *I've got to listen to him.* What an uncivilized scene!

Class cadre elections involve scheming, backstabbing, and bias from the teacher, but once they're elected, no teacher advises them, "You're in service to the students." Instead they'll say, "You have to lead them" or "You have to supervise them." God knows what kind of officials they'll make when they grow up, given all the tiny special privileges they've learned and been involved with from a young age.

In fact, with the exception of homework collection positions, the teacher should simply appoint the best tattletale as class president and be done with it.

THE PROBLEM WITH ENGLISH
2003

It's unfortunate that, due to reasons of historical and national importance, we're forced to learn a foreign language, and one regarded as greater in status than Chinese. I started learning English in the sixth grade, but for children nowadays, it's the earlier the better. When I started learning English, I asked anyone I could to teach me to say "I love you." I was innocent back then, you know. In junior high, students in the class started to ask around about how to swear and say dirty words. Even the older kids with bad English became very adept in this area and they developed a great interest for analyzing why Englishmen don't want to "fuck" their mothers but why the use of *bitch* is universal. A few years later, English turned out to be useful for talking to your girlfriend when your parents were around. Once the initial excitement wore off, I began to question whether English was granted too high a status.

We can't do anything about that, though. If foreign reserves were renminbi denominated, then we wouldn't need to learn English, or at least we wouldn't need to work so hard. When we walk, we think of the English word for *road*; when we eat, we think of the English word for *dinner*; and every school has an "English corner," and a select few in any group of Chinese people will discuss vulgar problems in English, such as: "How much is your gorgeous handbag?" (They haven't yet learned the sophisticated questions, such as: "Is this handbag real leather or nylon?") In the mornings, schools radiate English. You close your eyes and think you're in Oxford, but when you open them you realize you're in Tianjin.

Everyone says that your memory is best in the morning, but we've devoted this time to the language of another country.

We shouldn't blame anyone for this. School schedules are made with a purpose in mind. We're not learning English because it sounds good. Students have attained relative fluency in English, but not in Arabic, during their school years for business reasons on both sides.

I've always thought that the goal of learning was survival. Survival is a nice way of putting it; it's more about employment. Employers weigh you quickly by looking at your credentials; it's not a sign of all the knowledge you've accrued. Idiots all over the world have great credentials. English wouldn't be so important if we didn't want so many products from abroad and if it didn't make it easier to make money off foreigners. There are no other reasons. Maybe convenience, but it's such a tiny one. For these small reasons, too much time has been sacrificed.

Of course, for some students, English is a difficult and useless subject. *I* don't think it's useless, because it's impressive when anyone masters anything professionally. My qualm is that most people are unable to apply their English. I think it'd be awesome to be a really good English speaker, whether to talk to other people or to read books. My English is okay, although I stopped studying it after I dropped out. But now my English is better than it was at school, probably because I've watched all those foreign movies. All the branded English schools and other kinds of training courses these days are useless, of course. For parents and their children, the starting point is always job security, as if you could get hired just for speaking a few words of English. Interpreters may charge a lot these days, but they're still cheaper than prostitutes. If bosses can spend their money on that, then they can spend money on this.

I don't want to say something clichéd, such as "If you learn English in China, you're only learning grammar," but China *is* very rule-bound. In Chinese, "I want to buy one television," "To buy one television I want," "I to buy one television want," "I want to buy television one," and "One television I want to buy" all mean the same thing. So long as a television doesn't want to buy me, they're all correct. But strangely enough, people want to know which one is right and which one is wrong. I don't think I have the right to point out what's wrong in the way students learn English, but at the very least I can be skeptical of the emphasis on it.

The general view is that, even if you don't always need English in every office, it's used all the time in some offices. People prepare for the off chance, like girls who practice self-defense just in case. Isn't the price to pay for a "just in case" a bit too high?

We started learning a foreign country's language when we were young, then through three years of junior high, three years of senior high, and another four years at university, and we never doubted it for a moment. What can't you learn in ten years? If I studied bartending for ten years, I'd be the best bartender in the world, and I wouldn't earn any less than an interpreter. But in China, countless people have spent ten years studying English, reading in the morning and reciting in the evenings, but they're still at the same crap level. Why? Because we're doing something that completely betrays our environment. As for needing to converse in English with the flight attendant when we're on a plane, that's insane. What would happen if two Chinese people who spoke problematic English walked into a room? Still, I guess we could all practice our courage.

We're not bad students, and we can't blame the textbooks for our lack of an aptitude for English after ten years. If I'm at the racetrack and I need to turn a corner, I still know what to do even if I've forgotten my racing theory.

I once heard an "expert" on a television program say, "We can judge the moral quality of a Chinese person by their ability to speak English." What stupid crap. I'm embarrassed Chinese people can come out with crap like that, but the key thing was that the audience thought it really made sense. Perhaps they were numb, or maybe they were all in the process of learning English. I'd rather believe they were numb or had never thought seriously about the issue and never thought as children why they were studying English. If you don't believe me, go to a school now and ask the students. I don't think anyone would disagree.

Whoever came up with the notion that a country's moral character is determined by how well its people know the language of another country is an idiot. But this belief is widely held. It's implied when your friends know an English word you don't, and they mock you for it. It's also apparent when people admire an award winner who gives their speech in English, showing their superior moral character, even though the actor is facing a bunch of Chinese people. Maybe they prepared the speech the night before so they could say "Thanks for the recognition" in English. If they had used *encouragement* rather than *recognition*, the reaction would have been even more over-the-top. It's idiotic to speak English to a Chinese group. If you're keen to impress, why not speak Chinese to a group of foreigners, and go and say "Thank you" in Chinese when you win a Nobel Prize, a Grammy, or an Oscar? You don't have what it takes. When you have great English but choose not to use it, that's when you're good. Besides, so what if I don't speak great English; am I not allowed to be Chinese anymore?

I believe all kinds of people will say that, for all kinds of reasons, English ability is a measure of a person's moral character.

So in today's China an interpreter possesses the highest moral character.

There's nothing wrong with learning English. However, if you don't have any other skills, you'll end up an interpreter. If parents insist on getting their kids into interpreting, why not just send them abroad instead? Even if it's a big investment for a short period of time, they'll save themselves ten years of interpretation tuition. Then their kids can work for ten years as interpreters and earn their money back.

In the mornings, when I pass students in schools or kids riding bikes and reciting English, I get an odd feeling. There is an English corner in every school, but when I'm asking for directions to leave the city, some people don't even understand Mandarin. So please, let's popularize Mandarin first. We Chinese can't rely on English when we're asking for directions to the Great Wall.

IN THE KART EVERY DAY

Thrust into the role of antiestablishment rebel by his essays and comments critical of the education system, Han Han quickly tired of his early fame and the media caricature of a wild, backtalking teen prodigy. He found escape in a new challenge: racing. A fan of the sport as a child, he left Shanghai for Beijing in 2000 to pursue his dream, apprenticing himself to some of the best racers in China. Although he later characterized his writing from this period as slapdash efforts cobbled together to foot the bills, his novels and essays reflected being lost in a new city and the frustration of beginning a new career, which resonated with his younger readers. Frequent interaction with officials on the racing circuit provided new fodder for his satirical pen. Racing was more exciting than writing, but also made an interesting essay subject in and of itself, one that he returned to again and again.

THE PROBLEM WITH ME
2003

Three years ago I published *Triple Door*. Then I published *Minus One Degree*, *Go Like the Wind*, and *Poison*. Out of all my books, I like *Poison* the best. I like the language in *Go Like the Wind* best. I regret publishing *Minus One Degree* the most. I'm embarrassed to read that book. Even though it's been cut and edited, it was essentially a rushed book. Now I laugh at many of the essays and its internal contradictions.

Over a million copies of *Triple Door* have been printed to date. I'm surprised whenever I think of this. *Triple Door* is immature, with showiness that distracts from the plot. I wrote the book when I was a student, and lack of experience spurred me to work especially hard on the language, which gives it a certain style. Writing a novel like *Triple Door* was very difficult: There's not much plot, so the language had to be special, in each and every paragraph, and perhaps since writers in China are passionate about imbuing their novels with deep meaning, I'm unique. Meaning doesn't need to be imbued; just write what comes into your mind. If the whole novel is boring, then the meaning of the novel is that life is really boring.

Triple Door reached a certain height in terms of language, so surpassing it is very hard. Many people are certain I'll never surpass *Triple Door*. With this attitude, even if I wrote *Fortress Besieged*,* it'd be no good.

Fortress Besieged is a great work. It's the book that awakened me to how novels could be written. Literature is actually its own school of thought, and the best thing about literature is when it puts you in a certain mood. The second-best thing is when the writing is terrifically good, and the third-best is when writing carries a moral message. People say that in novels the words are just a carrier for extraordinary meaning, and if it's political meaning, then even better. Older Chinese writers often use phrases with no vitality, as if dead prose expresses great and lofty "humanity." This might be the perverted result of crushed official ambitions: When they write fiction they pretend they're writing summaries about departmental projects for major conferences. Otherwise, how do you explain the words being what they are?

I've been asked all sorts of immature questions. The worst was: "If you have to employ mathematics and physics in your writing, what do you do? You didn't get good grades in these subjects, so you're limited as a writer."

When you think about it, this might sound reasonable, but it's complete nonsense. First of all, who says I have to write about what I'm unfamiliar with? If a writer writes about an area he's unfamiliar with, but insists on doing so, he'll only

---

* Qian Zhongshu (1910–1998) is best known for his satiric novel *Fortress Besieged* (1947), one of the masterpieces of twentieth-century Chinese literature. The book follows the career of a literature student who returns from Europe to China with a fake degree to pursue a teaching career and seek a wife. The influence of the Qian's literary style and humor is evident in Han Han's early novels.

be a third-rate writer. Fiction is in essence all made-up. Why should I write about unfamiliar territory? Maybe you think I'm talking nonsense. But look at it like this: You like Jia Ping-wa's work,[†] but what if he started writing about racing? Of course that's impossible: Jia Pingwa would never write about racing. Even if he did, he'd do it in one sentence. Don't blame him if he can't tell the difference between Formula 1 and the World Rally Championship. Everyone leads a different life, with different interests, and these are the wellsprings of novels. As for subjects and disciplines, that's pointless worrying.

Back to the question at hand. "What do you do at your work unit?" I asked the guy.

He said he designed and developed software.

"What would you do if your boss's car broke and he asked you to fix it?" I asked.

"That wouldn't happen. There are other people," he replied.

That's how it is. Do only what you like and what you know how to. What you can't, other people will do. If you told me you knew how to do everything, I'd find something you couldn't do.

At the moment, what I do is race a dozen times a year. As a child I wished for this and finally the wish has come true. For a while I considered not writing. But training and racing had to be postponed because of SARS, so I wrote an essay collection, because I had nothing else to do.

[†] Jia Pingwa (born in 1952) is a best-selling author of earthy novels and short-story cycles of life in rural Shaanxi, and the recipient of a host of literary awards. *Turbulence* is available in English in a 2003 translation by Howard Goldblatt.

Once I was simply fed up with the educational system, and the essay I wrote about this ignited social debate. But I only expressed my dissatisfaction in a few thousand characters. Education is a huge issue, more than can be expressed even in ten thousand characters. I wrote down whatever came to mind, but it basically covered everything. I wrote it four years ago when I had just left school, and still felt a lot of hate, like someone recently divorced who hates everything about the other person. After four years he can think about it more calmly.

I'm done with talking about education. Just as when I wrote *Triple Door*, readers were delighted I was critical of the education system. They think my later work lacks that sharpness. I can't still be critical of the education system when I'm fifty. You can't keep writing the same thing for so many years. Furthermore, you can't keep demanding that a classmate who once delighted you by insulting your teacher talk only in insulting tones from then on.

I really like *Poison*. I think the content, the design, and the book itself represent how important I think the words are. Many people think that I'm a liar, as if I've put a gun to their heads, forcing them to buy the book. My books are never shrink-wrapped, and *Poison*'s preface says that it's a best-of collection, with only a few new pieces. Readers who have my books should just read the new pieces while standing in the bookshop. *Poison* is actually the product of narcissism, but no matter what others say, after I publish three more books I'm going to publish another best-of collection, and I'm still going to call it *Poison*.

Since there are so many pirated versions, when you're wondering if I've written a book, all you have to do is ask if Xinhua Bookstore has it in stock. If they don't, then what you have is pirated. Who knew that a state-owned enterprise could be useful?

As for piracy, I've in fact stopped caring. If my books are too highly priced in the future, I suggest you buy a pirated copy. But you'll need to bargain with the small booksellers: Get at least 20 percent off. Don't, under any circumstances, buy a pirated book at its original price. Pirate booksellers get theirs for as low as 30 percent of the cover price, so don't worry about them not making money.

When an afterword was needed for *Wire Copy*, I remembered the fiasco of *Minus One Degree*. I'd let someone else handle the book, so I didn't know that the editor in charge named on the back cover had no decision-making power. Thus a huge joke was born. Someone else was chosen to write the afterword. Specifically, they opined on what I did wrong and what I should do instead. The name of the piece was "Han Han, Think Again." It was totally silly: How can you get someone to insult the author in the afterword to his own book? This could only happen to me.

I didn't write the afterword for *Wire Copy*, either. I don't know the writer, but it's a piece that I really like, even though it's really an ad for the Mitsubishi FTO. I drive a Mitsubishi Lancer Evolution, also known as the Evo, the car that contends in the World Rally Championship. The Evo I drive was upgraded to the majestic Evo V, and now to the dwindling, eighth-generation Evo. On the road it has incredible acceleration power and the ability to turn corners like a roller coaster, but as soon as it's on the racing track it becomes useless. I use this example to illustrate the point that what you think of as extreme is actually very far from the most extreme.

I'm very far removed from leaving the elevated expressway on a motorbike and riding till the meter bursts, driving the Evo on Beijing's Third Ring at midnight at 230 or 240 kilometers per hour, and going to a leafy mountain road at noon to practice all-wheel drifting.

It's possible that I can write only when I have nothing else to do. I only remember to write after an event has happened, but I never do anything so that I can write about it.

IN THE KART EVERY DAY
Published in 2005

Practically every racer, whether formula or rally, started off in go-karts. That go-karts are for children because of their speed and safety is a lie. Kids ride them because they're small, and because they can reach the gas and brake pedals. Even so, a day at a crappy indoor track costs 500-plus yuan, and unless you're a paid driver, the sport can be very expensive. A lot of money has to be set aside by you or your parents, which may ultimately only result in proving that you're a terrible driver.

On the other hand, the go-kart track owner has it tough, too. Even though practicing at an indoor track is pricey for minors, the operators don't profit, either. The operators could easily have opened a bathhouse or karaoke joint instead of a go-kart track. The fact that they didn't is a credit to them. Still, the track near me in Shanghai was eventually converted into a bathhouse.

First, about the bathhouse that used to be an indoor kart arena. It's near the sea in Shihua. For a while I'd go there all the time to practice, irrespective of weather. I'd just left school, and I'd say it was the only venue for non-pornographic, non-gambling entertainment in the whole district. As I became better acquainted with the staff—or in other words, as I spent more money—I eventually learned which were the fast karts and which were the slow ones.

The tracks were simple designs, practically all of them

loopbacks. The karts were slow, and with no speed on the straightaways it all boiled down to waiting to corner. On that sort of track, it was easy just to drive to the end and then see who drove with the most precision.

Three of us dominated the top spots in the arena. One was a chubby teacher who no doubt didn't impress his students. The other contender, a man in his forties, was of unknown occupation and arrived on a motorcycle every day unhindered by wind or rain. Wind and rain didn't stop me because I drove. I was a published author by then, so of course they absolutely outclassed me.

We would push each other out of the lead. A scoreboard in the main hall in the arena showed that we three were at the top. The contest between me and my forty-something pals was fierce. The karts we drove were all very low-end, so we tended to drive a single kart. We would take turns driving, ravaging that one kart through the night, quite often until it broke down. The track had a huge clock that would put up your lap time. This meant that the one driving and the one watching were both nervous.

One of my competitors was an interesting guy. He had a son still in elementary school, and each time he was top ranked, he'd bring his son to watch the race. He'd let his son practice on his own, too, of course, but the main purpose of his visit was so he could watch his father destroy his opponents. But whenever my rival dropped in rank, his son had to stay home to do homework so that he could work hard at the track until he overtook me once more. Then the son would be back the next day, so that the boy would always think of his father as number one.

It used to be that, the evening before I went to Beijing, I'd head to the track and practice into the night, and if we went head-to-head, I'd manage to pull down the enemy due to my superior physical strength and financial power. But the record for fastest single lap kept getting pushed forward a few seconds because of the competition and the subtleties of the karts. It happened quite a few times that I'd have the quickest single lap before I left for Beijing and would leave happy and satisfied, but then when I returned I'd be informed that my record had been broken and that the teacher had gotten ahead of me as well. To stop more people from seeing that I'd fallen into third, I'd rush to the track without even dropping off my luggage at home. Sometimes the track wasn't even open or there was a private reservation, but I was a demanding customer and they'd open up early for me every time.

After a few hours of practice, I'd find that the kart seemed a little quicker than when I'd left. I'd ultimately make the fastest lap time and be listed in first place, but before long I'd be overtaken again, and when I couldn't make any more progress, the kart would speed up a little. It was a never-ending cycle.

Up until the last time. I went to Beijing for a while and came back to find that the track was now a bathhouse with "mid-range prices, high-end enjoyment" and "god-like pleasure." And the parking lot, where you could once park wherever you pleased, was now full of cars. Some people spend money on bathing and massages at a bathhouse but feel just as empty when they are done, and others spend the same to get a sore waist and a sweaty back, but they are totally satisfied.

The second kart track that made a deep impression on me was beneath the China Central Television (CCTV) tower in Beijing. My friend Pangzi ran it. It, too, was an immense investment for a minuscule return, so he survived by running a bar. Even though the karts were just as slow, the competition at this track was even fiercer, approaching international levels. It was probably the best indoor go-kart track in Beijing at the time, so it was pretty well-known. A Japanese was in first place; his name, with four characters, was very Japanese and pretty elegant. I pretty much felt that my life's dream was to overtake that guy.

In Beijing in those days a few friends and I practiced every night for months, and I finally passed the Japanese guy to win the glory of first place. The track's rankings changed every month, and whoever came out on top could easily have been a boss's boss or a worker's relative. But my performance was obvious to everyone.

Pangzi used to race motorcycles, but since he'd grown fat, the importance of the ratio of horsepower to weight meant he lost his advantage, and he switched to racing jeeps. He drove the earliest version of the Beijing BJ2020, one of those models that, after some time, you'd be able to pick up on the side of a street. Pangzi loved to brag, and he'd frequently come out with multiple versions of the same story because, over the course of bragging about it so much, he'd forgotten the thing itself. As far as go-karts went, he could instruct beginners, since, it was said, he himself had been a go-kart driver. We had a hard time imagining what he looked like in a kart: completely covering it, no doubt, looking like a Buddha floating along close to the ground.

Pangzi often crowed about his own wins and the passion with which he used to compete, and the most outlandish thing we heard was about the time he got injured. He said that he was thrown from the kart during fierce competition in the middle of a race, and the driver behind him ran right over him. We were all shocked, because kart wheels are about the size of a moon cake, and the kart itself covers only about a square meter and is just one centimeter off the ground. How could it run over Pangzi's nearly half-a-meter-wide body? If it really hit him, then I'm convinced that it would have stopped with a dull thud.

That Beijing track was where friends like Lao Su and I threw away a ton of time and money. It may have been the most basic of karting, but it was better than nothing, and it helped instruct me in car control and race lines. Regrettably, I never progressed to a professional indoor track, but I never got around to it because there wasn't any such place and because I'd already begun to race for real.

As a postscript, out of his love for bragging and racing (the two were inseparable), Pangzi was ultimately transferred to a track in Shenzhen, and took his northern legends to the south with him. And eventually the track itself was bought out and became a branch outlet of a large electronics chain.

A very long time later, I received a call one day inviting me to a track in the Shanghai suburbs to annihilate someone's record. I had to think about it for a while before it came to me that he was that dear old opponent who used to bring his son, and he had told me he'd found a new track somewhere. I sincerely hope that his son eventually becomes a top driver, with the sponsorship to put him through to high-level races. As for his dad, he didn't whore or gamble, he had goals despite being in his forties, and he frequently rode his motorcycle from one district to another for the chance of getting first place. I feel this means he was successful and happy.

MY FIRST TIME IN SHANGHAI
Published in 2005

After a winter-long preparation, everything was finally in place. Modifications to the car were complete. Even without parts like a racing computer or a differential, it at least had a roll cage, which meant it was ready to race. A rally race isn't like a track race, where the cars start simultaneously. In rallying, they start at two-minute intervals. Most of the spectators can see only one or two turns, and they can't easily distinguish between good and bad driving. So this is why we really loved the sport. If you know beforehand which turn (it's usually a turn) your boyfriends, girlfriends, and sponsors will be watching from, then once you get there you'll drive like hell. Flipping over won't even be a problem, since your friends, who have never witnessed a turnover, will now feel that their lives are more complete. If you don't flip or crash, that's excellent, of course: Everyone will think you're a fast driver. This applies even if you get back to the pit only to discover that you made the slowest time in the entire race, because then you can say, "I dodged a dog, my car broke down, I had an oil leak, and that's why I was slow."

They call this the uncertainty of rally racing. There are so many reasons why you're so slow that you don't have to use the same one every time. That's the uncertainty.

On television, you'll often see a good driver fail to place because of his mistakes, but he will never call them mistakes.

He'll just spread out his hands toward the camera and say, "Look, that's rallying." Just like how, in a track race, if you deliberately hit someone or knock someone out, you say, "Look, that's racing."

So, during my year of track racing, whenever two cars collided and one ended up knocked out, the thing I heard most was the remaining driver saying to the camera, "But that's racing." And then a group of pit repairmen would have to restrain the guy who was knocked out, and warn him, "Don't. You can't beat him."

They say the Chinese are at a disadvantage in contact sports, and perhaps Chinese people are a little worse at formula and track racing. Apparently the reason Ayrton Senna, the legendary Brazilian F1 racer, is so awesome is because if he sees someone blocking his way, especially when trying to pass him, regardless of whether or not it's legitimate, he'll charge into the pit after the race and rough him up, to beat out his opponent's arrogance. So if you happen to be in front of the guy during a race, you'd realize this, and also realize that the reporters and spectators are used to it, too—"Hey, that's just Senna"—and then you'd lose your confidence, and that's no good at all.

Clearly the Chinese are better suited to rally racing.

The team's choice to compete in rally was pretty insightful. It was our first race, and everyone was excited, from the owner to the car painter's wife. The race was on March 22, and since we would typically set off early, everyone headed out around March 15. The team was pretty impressive, and although it was a poorly equipped race car, the support team was marvelous. The new truck we had bought to serve as a repair truck broke down on the road, but the repair team following close behind was able to carry out some immediate fixes.

I had to do reconnaissance with Huang, another racer, so we set off a few days early. Driving from Beijing to Shanghai took more than ten hours along the highway I used most frequently. I had made more than ten round trips, so driving it was a piece of cake, and soon we were there. We arrived in the morning, because, as the team boss said, "Nighttime's more efficient for getting things done."

The first thing we did in Shanghai was find lodgings, and since the headquarters was at the Shanghai Gymnasium, we chose to stay at a nearby hotel. Huang and I hadn't seen much of the world, and we'd never seen what a raceway looked like, so we dragged the veteran navigator Guo Zheng with us to have a look. I knew the stage was in Sheshan, not far from my home, but I didn't know where the race would go. I had gone to watch it in 2002, but all I heard were some noises; I didn't see a single car.

We drove a civilian car to Sheshan and ate there. Parked along the roads were all kinds of private reconnaissance cars. In rally racing, private reconnaissance is strictly prohibited by the racing committee but is strictly carried out by all the drivers. It used to be particularly commonplace in the past, and people knew prior reconnaissance was forbidden; but since everyone did it anyway, no one was afraid of punishment; "If you catch me, I'll incriminate the others, and then there might be no cars left to race." So, as local fruit and vegetable farmers will tell you, prior to any race there are always sneaky people who drive around a lot, but they're not looking for violators of the one-child policy. Sometimes when they reach a turn they'll get out and take a look around, but they won't steal any vegetables. And the driver's always talking, and a secretary records things in a notebook next to him. What's the matter with that? That's rallying for you.

There are two race stages in Sheshan, both under ten kilometers, and run forward on the first day and backward the next. The road's narrow, and if a car's coming your way, you can't avoid a crash. We watched in fear the whole way, scared that someone from the auto federation would pop out of nowhere and say, "We've got you on camera. You were doing private reconnaissance, and your race eligibility is revoked." And then they'd add, "Your registration fee will not be refunded."

But I had come up with a countermeasure. I'd stand my ground and say, "Comrade, my home's inside this stage. I've got to use this road to go home every day."

And then they'd probably ask, "So what's the guy doing next to you, writing in a notebook?"

And I'd say, "You know I'm a writer. I'm dictating a piece and he's recording it. He's my assistant." And then Guo Zheng would look up and the auto federation guys would recognize him, and we'd have to flee the scene.

Fortunately, that never happened. We did pacenotes for the two stages, which we felt were unusually precarious. The road was entirely flat, but it ran along a river in some spots, and in other places there were walls and lots of little bridges. Guo Zheng said, "That's insignificant stuff. In the race at such-and-such, the mountains were high enough that if the car fell, it wouldn't hit bottom for half an hour." Huang and I didn't believe him. We'd always felt that Shanghai's raceway was the most dangerous. Of course, for cowards like the two of us, this meant that if our first race had been in mountainous Guizhou, we would have withdrawn from the race in fright during the reconnaissance.

Then we drove around Shanghai waiting for the arrival of the big teams, who finally showed up two days later. Then a display of race cars was set up in an open space at the gymnasium, where the teams showed off their cars for a full three days, with another day set up especially for media introductions. Throughout the entire media day, I saw fewer than one hundred spectators and less than ten media outlets—less traffic even than at the snack shop a hundred meters away. Nor did I spot the Shanghai media, who only care about F1, even though they can't distinguish between Formula Renault, F3, Campus, and F1. It's all the same to them.

This reminds me of something a reporter once said: "If the tires are exposed, it's F1." That means that when farmwork picks up, all the fields are hosting F1 races.

It's a process, of course, and totally understandable that reporters only report on the events they get paid for.

The atmosphere began to get tense ahead of formal reconnaissance. Fifty-odd race cars lined up and went through the four race stages in succession to make pacenotes. The race would be held on the second or third day.

At last the race was about to begin. I proved the excellence of my mental training, because on the day of the race I stayed sound asleep and someone else had to wake me up. I was totally clueless about everything from the checkpoints to driving lanes in the race stage. Fortunately, Guo Zheng was an old hand, and I only had to hear "Go," "Drive," "Stop," "Left," or "Right," and I was okay. Huang, a newbie navigator, got lost on Shanghai's elevated expressway but still managed to find his way to Sheshan in time for the race.

Although I was driving a Group N car, I started near the back because this was my first race. Ahead of me was a Team Giti Group N car, and ahead of that Master Xu from Shenzhen driving a Subaru that I heard was the reconnaissance car from the 1998 World Rally Championship. Regardless of what it once had been, in 2003 it was in pretty poor shape. My car, on the other hand, may not have had much in the way of modifications, but it was in pretty good shape because it hadn't taken part in any previous race.

The time came for me to enter the pit for the first time. Familiar faces were there already, and I received unprecedented treatment: As soon as I entered, someone handed me fruit and a towel, and then the car was jacked up to change tires, even though the four I was using were new. I guess they had to do something, since an idle pit crew wouldn't seem professional. The car's four new tires were quickly removed, and four identical new ones were put on in their place. Satisfied, I exuded confidence to everyone in the pit. Someone gave me chocolate and apples. If I got knocked out on the first stage, I wondered, would I have to return all the food? How could I face them again otherwise?

At last I pulled up to the starting line, right on time, and on seeing the two-minute countdown on the clock in front of me I got a peculiar feeling. This was the beginning of actual racing, in a totally unfamiliar place.

From the starting line of the first Shanghai stage was a straightaway nearly a kilometer long, a stretch of road on which the fastest race cars could get up to near maximum speed, but all that was in my mind was how I was going to pass through the turn ("left five, narrows, careful of guardrails on either side") after that. A dramatic skid or a perfect line? I reached the turn just as I made up my mind, but I couldn't brake in time and, sadly, missed it. Fortunately the straight road beyond it was closed off with only plastic tape or else I'd have smacked into a wall. So I had no choice but to back myself up.

Who would have thought that I'd turn out to need to back up at the first turn in my racing career?

But as luck would have it, I got out of the situation with just a warning, a cheap cost of around ten seconds off my time. The experience taught me that in a real race, at speeds approaching 200 kilometers per hour, it's hard to see precisely where a left-hand turn is, and driving in a helmet and four-point restraints feels totally different from normal. Also, the brake shoes of a car that's just started out haven't reached optimum working temperature. All of this informed me that a race car can't reach the extremes you'd imagine.

So I lost my nerve and drove listlessly over the next several kilometers, but even so the car felt unstable. Later, I learned that the instability was because I was driving too slowly. At a left in the final kilometer of SS1 (Special Stage 1), the exit of the turn was filled up with all the mud and gravel carried by the previous Group N cars. This is characteristic of the volatility of rally racing, and since I was using track tires whose surface was practically smooth, they lost their grip on the mud and skidded straight for the side of the road. A grove of trees stood at the roadside, one of which was enormous, but I figured I'd be more likely to bring misfortune on one of the many cute tiny trees standing beside it. Then there was a *bang*, and the side of the car whacked into a tree. *Damn,* I thought, *so the car's totaled.* Guo Zheng shouted, "Go!" and I thought he meant get out, and I almost undid my seat belt. Then he shouted, "Hit the gas!" and without thinking I put it in gear and drove off.

At the finish line, I said to him, "The car's okay?" since it was my first crash and I didn't know how badly a car could get wrecked. In my mind, Guo Zheng's side of the car had been totally destroyed. He said, "It's no big deal. It's not really a crash. Last time I was with ———, we flipped a few times in an accident, but after getting it back upright we raced normally and made —— place."

"Shit, I thought we'd have to withdraw," I said.

When I got out and had a look, there was a dent only the size of a finger. The car was sturdy, and besides, the tree was pretty small. So I asked him, "What about if I'd hit that huge one?"

"No difference. You'd still drive away," he said.

Then it was on to SS2, which was half gravel; and while the other cars were changing into rally tires, with my skills and boldness I elected to use track tires. Of course, the real reason was my team's lack of experience: We didn't have rally tires. So naturally I was slower than ever, at least forty seconds off, and could have driven the not-particularly-slow gravel stage entirely in first gear.

Finally, I could get back to the pit. Lacking any equipment, the task in the pit, as far as our team was concerned, was changing tires and giving the drivers food, since we had no way to deal with problems, even small ones like a water tank leak, an intercooler leak, or a snapped shock absorber.

This was the team's first race, and I sensed that the pit crew was more nervous than I was. The team boss and manager had high hopes, too, but were afraid that they'd watch me leave the pit and wouldn't see me come back again. They were overjoyed to see me, and naturally I was a little dazed as well. I felt not only that I'd succeeded in driving forward into the pit but that the race itself was over, and I accepted their congratulations. I reveled in the joy of the pit, and then Guo Zheng shouted, "Time's up!" and we had to leave again.

And then it was another race like the first one, only this time, in SS3, the car ahead of me had to withdraw, so running right ahead of me was that Shenzhen driver. Even with two minutes between starts, within thirty seconds I'd already caught up to him, and since the stage was so narrow, I couldn't pass and had to stay on his tail all the way to the finish line.

He blocked me for a long time, but Master Xu was down-to-earth, and apologized to me in the pit, saying that his daughter and his daughter's friend really liked me, which instantly dissipated any thoughts of violence. It occurred to me that it couldn't be easy for him, infatuated with racing and trying it for the first time at his age in such a poor car. So I said, "No problem, no problem. Go ahead and block me."

And so I was blocked until the conclusion of the first race day. Back at the hotel I learned that I'd placed eighth or ninth in Group N.

That night everyone was excited. There were so many Group S3 cars that Huang's position was practically invisible, but for better or for worse everyone was still there after that day's race, and the cars hadn't suffered much. All four were still all-wheel drive, and the Jetta was still a sedan.

At the meeting that night, the team started handing out new tasks, the general idea being that we all had to maintain today's slow pace and see if any racers ahead of us would experience a miserable withdrawal.

The atmosphere was far more relaxed the following day, and, as hoped, the racers up in front withdrew for various reasons, as if our team was issuing collective curses rather than sitting idle while we were racing. Cars are like that in a race: When a driver ahead of you drops out, even though you may feel superficial regret, in your heart you're always secretly happy that their withdrawal means your rise in rank. Huang was a big adherent, so when he raced he had an enjoyment that other drivers didn't share. Other drivers found joy through good performance in the union of man and machine, but Huang found pleasure in dropped-out cars on the roadside. Huang's happiness was everywhere. For the rest of us, if a car dropped out, it was either ahead of us or behind us:

Longyou is a county seat with an impressive name that seems recognizable to all who hear it even though no one really knows what province it's in. Its fame comes from a grotto, the same Longyou Grottoes that the local government continually publicizes. *Oh, right, that's where the Longyou Grottoes are!* you think. When I thought about it later, something seemed a little off, but understanding only came at daybreak: I'd been thinking of the far more famous Longmen Grottoes, which are in Henan.

The government of Longyou attaches high importance to the caves, and has affirmed repeatedly that since they have no idea of how these caves were formed, it's truly a miracle of nature that's too difficult for science to explain. This leads one to suspect that the caves were secretly dug out with government funding.

The entry fee to the Longyou Caves is 50 yuan. It's suitable for summer tours, for apart from the coolness there's nothing else special about it. But the government insists that it's the Ninth Wonder of the World. And really, why not? The world has eight recognized wonders, so everything else is number nine.

But we rally drivers like Longyou because it has an excellent track, a natural track that, turns included, has no side drop-offs, which means that you can skid out and then, with the help of local police, you can be pushed back on again.

The Beijing Top Speed Racing Club reached Longyou early, and soon saw signs of the race. Banners on the road welcomed the competition, reading: "Spicy Grandpa's Poached Fish Welcomes the National Auto Rally Tournament to Longyou" on the front, and on the back: "Everything 20% off during the race; alcohol and soft drinks full price," as well as congratulations from every department of the local government and from every local factory. The banner makers, most of whom were hoping to witness fabulous crashes, wrote against their conscience, "May racers from all parts of the country perform well and depart satisfied."

Banners were hung at the door of practically every hotel on nearly every street, and along the side of country roads. A banner up top read "From XX Village, Best of Luck to the Auto Rally Race," and below that was: "Don't leave school in search of work; finish classes just in case." From the way they rhymed, it felt like they were originally one banner, reunited after years of separation.

We stayed at the newly built four-star Longyou International Hotel, where the rally association had set up its headquarters. Practically all the rooms in Longyou were booked. Next to the hotel was a nightclub called Earthly Paradise. The fame of Beijing's Earthly Paradise club, and the way its stories grew ever more incredible as they were passed around, meant that every city in the country had a nightclub with that name—or if they didn't, it was because the name had been snapped up by a bathhouse.

I'm convinced that the people happiest about the rally race were the local hostesses. They're what a racing team does for fun wherever it goes, so whenever they arrive at a place, the price of the ladies goes up along with everything else, keeping the government and the local madams busy at hospitality. The government gives the rally committee money to hold the race, and the teams return some of that money to the locals in a different guise, through prostitution, letting it accumulate bit by bit in a truly beneficial cycle.

Around midnight we went out for a snack. I took a spin through Longyou and discovered that the place had lots of well-known franchise eateries; the county town turned out to be bustling. Transportation was a mess, though. Every car seemed to have left the factory absent low beams, leaving their high beams switched on constantly, dazzling each other from five hundred meters away. If a ditch lay in the road some-where in that five hundred meters, both cars would surely fall in. And the taxis—forget about them stopping on a whim, because the drivers liked to talk standing beside each other. The most impressive I saw was five cars stopped in a line at night, totally blocking the road. With the idea the five cars had caught the race bug and were seeing who could start fastest, I pulled up to watch; but after standing there five minutes, I realized they were just chatting. At the time I thought: *What if the driver of the first car had something to say to the driver of the last one? How long would it take to pass the message?*

I laid on the horn for a while, but they didn't seem to want to make way. A dragon can't take on a snake in its element, so I let it go and did a U-turn. The drivers stuck their heads out the window to watch me, probably thinking, *That racer has no manners, blowing his horn in the middle of the night.*

After three days of easy relaxation, registration formally began. Around this time SARS had begun wreaking havoc in Beijing. We were worried that we wouldn't be able to get back after the race, because there were all kinds of rumors, some of them incredible exaggerations.

With cities across China in a state of high anxiety, we were thankful to be worry-free, amusing ourselves in a small city in the south.

Registration finished quickly, and the next day was devoted to reconnaissance. Pacenotes took half a day to finish. We were extremely impressed with the road and safety arrangements and looked forward to getting on with the race.

We visited various places during the day to eat, get foot massages, take walks, and wait for the race to begin.

That night, the managers of the major teams were called to the race control center for a meeting. We had been discussing who would lead and who would follow during the second day of inspections, and then someone said, "Do you think the race will be canceled?"

I said, "Not likely. There's no SARS in the south, right?"

Other people said that it wasn't easy getting all the cars and people here, and since the hotels were booked, the pacenotes made, and the ladies visited, how could they simply cancel the race?

Ten minutes later we received word that the race had been canceled due to SARS, and all major race teams had to leave Longyou before dawn the next morning. Angrily, we began packing up, completing our weeklong holiday; and as the curtain of night descended, several hundred transport cars, repair cars, racing cars, reconnaissance cars, and VIP cars took to the Hangzhou–Quzhou Expressway and then dispersed along other highways to return to their hometowns, where they had their temperature checked at the tollbooths and were even observed in quarantine before being released. We waited nervously for SARS to pass.

When the race resumed three months later, it skipped over Longyou and Beijing and moved on to Changchun. The Longyou race was postponed until the end of the year, before the Asia-Pacific Rally Championship. Later I realized what a fortunate postponement this was, because the team had swapped the large calipers on the front brake for a small brake caliper better suited to the gravel roads of the rally race, but they hadn't swapped out the rear ones, since those were small calipers already. Back in Beijing we realized that since the rear calipers exceeded the expected dimensions, it prevented the installation of fifteen-inch rims. Without SARS, race day would have arrived before I discovered that I had no rear wheels. Mine would've been the first car to withdraw from the Longyou stage, and I'd have done it in the pit without even racing, unable to attach my wheels.

ACTUALLY, I'M A WRITER
2010

My girlfriend went to a prestigious high school that I couldn't get into, so I tried hard to develop what I was good at. Around that time I discovered I could run really fast. I got into the best high school in town based on that.

I should say that there was something else: The other thing I could do well was writing. I didn't want to do it during my fun time, so I sacrificed school hours.

I failed many of my classes in senior high because I overestimated my intelligence: I thought in a month or two I'd catch up. But I discovered that senior high math, physics, and chemistry were very different from junior high math, physics, and chemistry. I gave up.

It was only a matter of time before I was going to get kicked out, so I left on my own before that happened. The teachers told me not to harm society after I left, and asked me what I planned to live on. Royalties, I replied. The teachers sniggered at this. I had no choice but to snigger along with them.

I received my first royalties in Beijing.

That was when thirty thousand copies of *Triple Door* were printed, and I received 30,000 yuan. I didn't have enough to buy a car. Once the first print run had sold out, the printers added another twenty thousand copies. *That's 50,000 yuan!* I thought happily. I thought about the kind of car I could buy, but market research told me cars cost more than 50,000 yuan, so I set my eyes on something secondhand.

They added a further fifty thousand copies. One hundred thousand yuan! Citroën Fukangs and VW Santanas and Jettas, and their powerful capabilities dominated the Internet forums. I couldn't afford any of the best three out there. The Beijing BJ2020 wasn't bad, but I didn't know how much it cost. There were no official Web sites at the time where you could check prices. A Beijing Jeep had to be at least 100,000 or 200,000 yuan, I thought, so I waited.

When a further two hundred thousand copies had been printed, I stuffed the cash in a rucksack and went to a car dealership. In a quavering voice I asked them how much the Beijing BJ2020 was. It was just over 40,000 yuan. Suddenly, I hesitated, and I decided not to get it. People can be really cheap: I'd have bought it for 190,000 yuan.

I looked over the other cars. A Jetta wouldn't do: In the northeast they were used as taxis. Santanas were used as taxis in Shanghai. No way was I going to drive a taxi. I had to be unique, so I chose a Fukang. I drove it to Beijing to get it modified, and then . . . as soon as I got there, I discovered Beijing taxis were fucking Fukangs.

I joined a Shanghai racing team, Shanghai VW 333, the best team in the country at the time. The owner didn't need me to do well, since I was good publicity for them.

That racing car was the first I drove seriously, and that year . . . I won two races. After winning lots and lots of races, if I finally win a championship that I'm satisfied with, I'll be overjoyed and will announce to everyone: "Actually, I'm a writer."

LITERATURE AND THE ERA OF MICROBLOGS

In his downtime between races, Han Han kept a blog. By 2008 he had overtaken film star Xu Jinglei as China's number one blogger. While critics could write off Han Han's early novels and essays as the work of a young punk with no sense of literary history, his blog posts made clear that he kept up with contemporary literature and was conscious of following in the tradition of Chinese satirists such as Qian Zhongshu.

Han Han's writing had always been humorous, his trademark style deft and easy to read; but in blogging he began to address increasingly weighty topics, particularly in the run-up to the 2008 Beijing Olympics. The more excitable media outlets compared him to 1920s intellectual Lu Xun, despite his protestations, as he viewed Lu Xun as too unsympathetic and argumentative. Which isn't to say Han Han had become buttoned down: He remained ever the troublemaker, no stranger to flame wars, and he seldom shied away from a good debate. Print collections of his posts became best sellers, propelling him to even greater prominence. Newspapers and magazines began to interview him about the contemporary Chinese literary scene.

As the era of blogs gave way to that of microblogs like Sina Weibo and WeChat, Han Han made the transition himself, and his blogging output drastically declined in 2013. But his wit and humor are well-suited to the 140-character format, and his posts are still often quoted and frequently go viral.

WHY ARE THERE STILL MODERN POETS?
September 26, 2006

> *These posts are Han Han's contribution to an online furor over the meaning and value of poetry sparked when forum commenters discovered the work of Hubei-based contemporary poet Zhao Lihua, whose simple language and everyday subject matter inspired by poets like Wallace Stevens provided ample material for Internet users to parody and ridicule. Zhao called Han Han's posts "impetuous and insolent" and said that getting involved in online flame wars was a waste of his talent.*

For the past few days, people have been arguing online about the definition of poetry. Weird, I thought, but didn't read any of it. My view has always been that modern poets and poetry have no reason to exist, and that modern poetry as a genre is meaningless. Paper is expensive these days, so why not write prose all on one line? The good thing about classical poetry is that it has poetic form, but form is not a limitation. To gain an audience, a car racer has to drive within a designated lane. Start driving any way you like, and you're not far from our current traffic situation: The audience can pretty much drive however they please, so why would they need to watch *you*? That's why poetry has degenerated to what it is now. It's no longer poetry, but poets still think that's what they're writing.

Writing prose is writing prose, but when it comes to getting young female literati into bed with you, *prose writer* isn't as effective as *poet*. Perfectly fine punctuation is right in front of you, but you won't use it. First you cramp up your brain, then cut the sentence in half, mince it into a paste, then line up the characters randomly, like in a lottery. They really think they're artistes. And don't go bringing up Xu Zhimo's "Softly I am leaving . . ." and Hai Zi's ". . . with spring blossoms,"* since of course you'd expect a few flowing lines out of decades' worth of writing. But, overall, the existence of modern poetry only has value as lyrics to a handful of songs. Without any poetic forms, then lyricists are sufficient. What do we need poets for?

This has been my opinion since I saw a collection of modern poetry in the school library, and I'll never change it. If the practice questions in a math exercise book were set out like modern poetry, you would have plenty of room to show your work. In every single one of my novels, I've not forgotten to ridicule modern poetry, and then include a poem of my own, which some clueless readers take to mean that I actually like the stuff. So today I've said it more bluntly. Finally, I'm going to compose a modern poem:

---

* Xu Zhimo (1897–1931) is China's foremost modern poet; this line is the opening to his most famous poem, "Good-bye Again, Cambridge." Hai Zi (1964–1989), one of China's most famous contemporary poets, tragically killed himself at the age of twenty-five. "Facing the Sea, with Spring Blossoms" is one of his best-known poems.

A SMALL POEM

"Stiff Neck on an Airplane"

Small
or poem
one poem or two poems
my neck
really
really hurts
did
I get a stiff neck sleeping on the airplane
or did
the airplane get a stiff neck from me
he says
to write
prose
pro
pro prose
don't forget
to use punc-
tuation

Yuh

POETS ARE DESPERATELY NOT WRITING POETRY
September 28, 2006

To be honest, I'm not such a big fan of modern poets. The modern poet has only to master one skill: the enter key. The difference between this most recent batch of poets and the earliest ones is that they don't even have a sense of social responsibility. The title *poet* is a means of escape from their messed-up, degenerate lives. After all, the vast majority of other skills are earned through labor; what's easy is writing vertical contemporary poetry.

> *Am*
> *I*
> *right*
> *?*

I read essays by two poets today that demonstrate that once poets go beyond the contemporary poetry structure, their logic is breathtakingly messed up. Of course, this also fully demonstrates that their essays and poems share the same lineage. Setting aside the dirty language of pure poets, from an appreciation of their writing style alone we can understand why they can only write poetry: They aren't able to write anything else.

Poets always imagine that outsiders or the general public

can't simply talk about music and poetry, that they're all fools who don't understand. They feel that Internet commenters are only superficially imitating Zhao Lihua's line breaks, but can't imitate her wisdom and philosophical connotations. And that the parodists are shameless and ignorant of poetry. I suggest we remove all the line breaks from Zhao Lihua's poems and then let her rebreak them again and see if she ends up with the originals.

What I can't understand is why, as poets, they don't attack me with what they do best: poems. It turns out that when poets get desperate, they, too, lapse into plain talking. Are these great modern poets just not powerful enough? Of course, maybe a poet would shoot back that attacking in modern poetry would sully its wonderful innocence. But then you can't go off and lay waste to another form of writing, not even how-to guides. My personal advice is that poets should write poems in refutation to show off the omnipotent glory of modern poetry.

Am
I
right
?

MODERN POETS GET ORGANIZED
October 3, 2006

Poets have started organizing, and I've heard that they've held poetry reading sessions to talk about the situation. I thought that poets were isolated, but as it turns out, they like to get together into groups, too! Through analyzing the language that groups of poets use, I found that poets all share a few characteristics:

1. **They think only *they* can discuss poetry.** All of you ordinary folk are only allowed to say that poetry is good, which puts you in a subordinate position to worship it. If you say that it's bad, it's over for you, even if you're some kind of leading industry figure: Your moral quality, intelligence, and education will all be questioned.
2. **Poets think that they're superior to other people.** They're standing on the top of a tall, tall mountain, looking down on us, the stupid ones. Of course, if you're worshipping them and you're a young literary woman, you're already halfway up the mountain.
3. **Poets think that you have to have very high ideals to read or write poetry.** Basically, only the poets can accomplish this. And that's why they communicate only among themselves.

That's pretty much everything. Why do I feel that if I joined a gang of poets, it would be like joining a cult where every member has lost their soul to the dark arts? The poets are superior to us, of course. We just need to plant both feet firmly on the ground. String yourself up and you're higher than me, too, but there's nothing I can do about that.

Some poets even imagine that problems with my "awareness and moral character" are due to me never attending university. Are poets so clueless? Is this their open thinking? Modern poetry may look free-form, but how did poets end up so narrow-minded? Truly, the freer you are, the more limited you become.

Several years later, in June 2010, Han Han apologized to Zhao Lihua and other poets: "My viewpoint three years ago was incorrect, and I feel ashamed for the misunderstandings and harm I caused you all. Out of pride I never said anything. I hope for your forgiveness and understanding."

WANG SHUO
January 2007

I got calls from a few media outlets today. The general idea was that *Sanlian Life Weekly* did a feature on Wang Shuo, and then they tried to use some of his views to incite an incident. It's a shame I'm a fan of both Wang Shuo and *Sanlian Life Weekly*. How will they cause an incident now?

The journalists were rookies. "Wang Shuo said the post-'80s generation is a bunch of so-and-sos. What do you think?" they asked.

"I wholeheartedly agree," I replied. "I think so, too."

There are some very neurotic people in China who have no sense of self-mockery. As soon as something negative is said about their city or their group, they immediately go crazy. I once made some remarks about girls from the Shanghai International Studies University, and all at once a bunch of people went insane. Did they have scholarships from that university, or was it something else? Didn't they all get there by testing in, and would have ended up elsewhere if they screwed up? Normally, you can say however many negative comments you like in private about your own school or city, but if someone else makes those same comments, for some reason you've got to defend your little pile. That's not honor. That's stupidity.

If someone makes a negative comment about Chinese car racing, I'd be overjoyed. An outsider says something that we can't say ourselves very easily. If you're thinking clearly, you ought to realize how fortunate you are.

Wang Shuo is a writer I really admire. He's a rare Chinese writer who has actually written decent work. He's said he's uneducated, but that's because he wants to lower himself to the ground floor so he can criticize the people upstairs, and then when there's an emergency and everyone has to jump out of the building, he'll be hurt the least. The key thing is that some people don't get this and think he's really uneducated. Wang Shuo has made the biggest contribution of any individual to Chinese film and television series. *In the Heat of the Sun* is the best film—not one of the best, *the* best—ever made in China. No justification is necessary for the television series. The Chinese are very particular about modesty, but can't you tell when someone is being overly modest?

When Wang Shuo debates, he almost never mentions his work but argues with his opinions rather than using his novels to shut people up. But so many fucking idiots lay out the line that he's just making a play for money or groupies. The truth of it is that Wang Shuo expresses his opinions extremely modestly, yet many people come out with all sorts of crazy things. When Wang Shuo says he isn't educated, he's already insulting you, but he's keeping it deeply hidden. Like if Olympic hurdler Liu Xiang said he couldn't run very fast, he'd really be calling everyone else turtles. Wang Shuo has produced classics—lots of them. In China, someone with awesome work who hasn't been dubbed a master has got to be good, and regardless of how his next novels turn out, he's done enough already.

Yet even some "post-'80s" writers think he should "set a literary example, and not act recklessly." Is this something that a fucking twenty-something writer should be saying? If you didn't know better, you'd think they were in a government work meeting. For a real writer, recklessness is very important. When you're so young you should have courage, since, for the time being, society has not yet forced conflict or hardship upon you—but all you've learned to write are weak essays on your knees. When the wind rises, you won't be able to stand straight, and if it keeps blowing, you'll be reduced to cannon fodder. When I saw those opinions, it was too late for me to pretend I didn't know the people saying them. Should I help you out just because I was born roughly around the same time as you? Do we have to join the same club? I've only heard of people joining the same Party if they happen to have the same aspirations and interests, but I haven't heard that people born around the same time have to join the same gang. If I'd known that much, I'd have sunk low enough to enroll in college long ago.

So here's some advice for media outlets with a conscience: Unless Wang Shuo somehow hurts my family or takes my woman, the scene you're waiting for will never happen. Especially since by that point only a fucking idiot would have time to write an essay.

THERE HASN'T BEEN ANY RENAISSANCE

Interview with Southern Metropolis Weekly
November 2012

Rejuvenation Is the Problem, Not the Arts

SWeekly: How do you understand "renaissance"?

Han Han: When I started the magazine *Chorus of Soloists*,* its first name, *Literature and Arts Rejuvenation*,† didn't get approved. No new magazines with *literature and arts* in the title would be approved, they said. I believed them and substituted my first backup title. But then a lot of magazines appeared with *literature and arts* in their names, like *Literature and Arts Stylistic Appreciation*,‡ and at last I understood that *literature and arts* wasn't the problem. *Rejuvenation* was.

The term *renaissance* is generally associated with Italy, but I think in the minds of Chinese people, literature and

---

* This magazine bore the English name *Party* and was compelled to shut down after one issue in 2010.

† The European Renaissance is rendered in Chinese as *wenyi fuxing*, a term that directly translates as "literature and arts rejuvenation."

‡ This magazine, edited by novelist and publisher Guo Jingming, bears the English title *ZUI Found* and caters to a young adult and college-age audience.

arts rejuvenation may be associated with a period in the 1930s that seems to exhibit signifiers of rejuvenation: a little bit of enlightenment activity and a little bit of top-notch literature. After that there was a drop-off. The Internet has helped the development of literature and arts, but it's still pretty far from a "rejuvenation" or a "flourishing."

SWeekly: Is China likely to achieve a renaissance under the current system?

Han Han: The system is fictitious. It's a mental construct. Whether literature and arts can be revived is a mental problem. If there's no mental rejuvenation, additional funding and slogans are of no use. Sometimes—I'm fairly pessimistic—the past is past. The era of pen pals, the era of hand-copied manuscripts, the era when rock was big, and the golden age of Hong Kong film—they're gone and they're not coming back.

SWeekly: Do you trust people's minds now?

Han Han: (*Laughs.*) Emotions are what people trust now. People follow their emotions, regardless of right and wrong. What matters is what looks good and what sounds nice.

SWeekly: Can a system be constructed if everyone follows their emotions?

Han Han: It's hard. Really hard. The system is enormous, and lots of the visible people are morons. But, given how large the system is, there are actually quite a few elite, clever people in its service.

SWeekly: You're pretty pessimistic.

Han Han: Right. Like I said, the past is past. But you've got to try your best to accomplish things. It's hard today for literature and arts to thrive like it used to because the medium has changed. When I did the magazine, I wanted to make it a place that brought attention to the creative work of young people. Everyone wants to be famous, but without a suitable medium to achieve that, they're liable to play to the masses, which means no one will be interested in our serious interviews.

Repeat Enlightenment

SWeekly: Are you optimistic about the era of microblogs?

Han Han: In small terms, from a purely literary point of view it doesn't matter whether a renaissance is hard or easy. In a larger sense, if you understand it as "human awakening," a problem crops up: repeat enlightenment. In the Internet age you may see things spread quickly, but it's still hard, since the audience is always the same, I've noticed.

If there are two million people in an enlightened audience, then enlightenment is always carried out among that same two million people. It's difficult to break down the barriers and reach the people who like Super Girls like Yico Tseng and Chris Lee,§ or American television. . . .

---

§ Super Girl was a phenomenally popular *Idol*-style reality singing competition that drew an audience of 280 million for the finale

Renaissance, or personal awakening, becomes just another TV drama. Your people like *Desperate Housewives*, but my people like *Renaissance*. That's what it turns into, and the barriers extend pretty far. Microblogs managed to obtain a degree of free expression, but the more the intellectuals spoke, and the more they fought among themselves, the faster their credibility declined—faster than the government's, even.

SWeekly: What's responsible for the decline in intellectuals' credibility?

Han Han: Many factors can be found in the intellectuals themselves. First, no consensus, and second, no joining forces. It's like, say, we're all on the same bus going to the same place but we need to stop for gas, and I say we should save money and refill with 93 octane, but someone else says we need to be driving faster, so we should refill with 97 octane. And then someone more extreme says the vehicle should have 98 octane fuel so that it can drive as fast as possible straight to the destination. As a result, even though the three of us want to go to the same place, we start fighting and blow up the gas station, and then a group of people gathers to laugh at us idiots. That's an easy situation to get into these days.

Microblogs look like they can change lots of things, but that's very difficult in practice. In the era of traditional media, you've had newspapers that were actually able to change things. They changed systems and trends, and

---

of its second season in 2005, won by Chris Lee. Yico Tseng was a runner-up in the 2009 season.

even the fates of some officials. But attention shifts so rapidly in the microblog era that significant public issues may last just a day or even half a day. And as forces are gathering, if some idiot comes out shouting, attention will be diverted.

SWeekly: Is there any way to break down those barriers?

Han Han: It's hard. The only way is through the earliest basic education, since education is the strongest barrier of all. Our children are in a deplorable education system.

When a class of fifty-odd students is given a question, for example, twenty-five of them might not care at all, and twenty will accept the brainwashing. Only four or five of them will have any personal awakening. A lot of people we know might have an opinion about a certain person, and strongly dislike him because we think he's done a lot of bad things, but when you ask around at a reunion of your classmates, you may find out that you're the only one among them who feels that way. That's why I think that breakthroughs in education have to start as early as possible.

I want to edit textbooks for my children and self-publish them. A friend's got a few publishing plans, and I want to publish new extracurricular materials, but approval is impossible to obtain.

Second, reliance on science. The little freedom and flexibility we've gained is actually convenience brought to us by technology; without it, I believe we'd still be mired in an era of alternating restrictions and relaxations. You might be able to criticize the Three Gorges Dam right now, but only because the forces behind its construction have lost power. This is not free expression but an outlet for speech opened up by a power struggle. There's nothing optimistic about that.

SWeekly: To you, when were China's recent eras of literary prosperity?

Han Han: The May Fourth period and the 1980s. The former had freedom, the latter had passion.

Mutual Disdain Among Literati

SWeekly: You have to admit that, set against Soviet literature from the same period, our authors come off weak by comparison. What do you think is the reason for this?

Han Han: It's dictated by differences in national character, for one thing, and for another, to many Soviet writers, Europe was their backyard. That is, when they were persecuted in the USSR, they could find shelter in many places in Europe and continue to write. And, like many countries in Europe, they belonged to the Indo-European language family, so their languages had a lot in common. Another reason is that Chinese people sometimes won't acknowledge their own. A Chinese person doing the same thing as a foreigner may subconsciously feel like an outsider. It's an extension of Empress Dowager Cixi's dictum, "Better to grant to foreign powers than give to house slaves," and contributes to our own mutual contempt. A tragic combination of factors, including time, personality, language, and ethnicity, forms what we are today.

SWeekly: What, apart from their environment, do China's writers and artists lack in themselves? How large do you think the gap is compared to contemporary foreign literature?

Han Han: They're not lacking in themselves. They lack readers, they lack high royalty payments, and they lack social insurance. Our social transformations and our writing are both unique. I advise against comparing our contemporary literature against foreign literature.

SWeekly: Among the Chinese authors you've had contact with, what problems bother you the most?

Han Han: Mutual disdain among literati. Early on, I had the tendency to look down on other writers and dismiss their writing and thought my ruthless, unsupported comments were pretty good. It's a back-and-forth disdain that can easily turn to mutual slander. Some people think there's a strong cliquishness among Chinese writers, but that's understandable, since people have the freedom to make their own friends.

SWeekly: How useful have ideas been in rejuvenation of literature and arts? If China wants to achieve a renaissance, does it have a greater need for ideas or for courage?

Han Han: There hasn't been any renaissance. This age is so full that even if a renaissance were to arrive, followed by a new industrial revolution, we wouldn't immediately be aware of it. As for ideas, let's not get carried away.

SWeekly: What's meant by *young writers* right now is those born in the '70s, '80s, and '90s. Compared to those born in the '50s and '60s, the new generation seems to have matured late, and is quite far from producing work that can contend with classics of contemporary literature. Why is that?

Han Han: I'll grant you that lots of writers born in the '50s and '60s have written lots of outstanding work, but people have a tendency to look back at the past without acknowledging the present. Someone will eventually make the observation that the writers born in the 2020s and '30s may sell well and are quite popular but, compared with the group born in the '80s and '90s, they don't seem to have anything that can contend. . . .

SWeekly: Some academics believe that history is missing from post-'80s literature. What's your view?

Han Han: I'm aware of lots of younger writers who have done quite a bit of historical depiction. When it comes down to it, what some academics actually mean when they say there's an absence of history in the work of young writers is that younger writers aren't setting their work in the Cultural Revolution, the Great Leap Forward, the Anti-Rightist Campaigns, Rustication, and other special periods that they themselves experienced. Honestly, even though I've got a rough idea of that period of history, I wouldn't have the courage or confidence to set essays or a novel in a special time in the history of human civilization that I never experienced. Besides, with most of the witnesses still alive, it's easy for young writers to make fools of themselves. It's hard for someone who didn't go through that era to understand it. It's also obvious that if a young writer does write about that era, certain academics will leap up and mockingly say that young authors should live in the moment and write about their own lives and their own time period, and that it's inadvisable to write about the peculiar experience of their fathers' generation, and point out tons of holes: "Look, it wasn't like that at all back then. . . ."

SWeekly: Since the turn of the century, literature by authors born in the '80s has been given the marketing label *youth literature*, obscuring that generation's more outstanding, serious literary creations.

Han Han: Literature is literature. Youth literature, serious literature, and even time travel romance, palace intrigue, and science fiction are all part of it. There's no such thing as "more outstanding, serious literary creations." In literature, there's only good and bad. Good reads and bad reads. Of course, the criteria for judging the good from the bad varies from person to person.

From Beijing Youth Weekly
July 2012

On Writing

BYW: You carry a lot of labels: "young author," "driver," "public intellectual," "opinion leader," "citizen," and even "public enemy." How do you view these labels, and which do you accept or reject?

Han Han: Different media outlets have different personalities, so I've been slapped with all kinds of labels. I'm covered in them like a steamer trunk. But what can I do? I won't reject them, since that might come off as fussy. A driver, sure. A writer . . . I wasn't willing to call myself that before 2008, especially since my novels prior to *Chaos in Chang'an* were marked by excessive imitation—of Qian Zhongshu, for example—and I didn't have a style of my own. But I feel like I rate as an author post-2008. My writing has crossed that threshold, and isn't all that bad, if I do say so myself. My work after *Chaos in Chang'an* has its own style that's not an imitation of anyone else's.

BYW: Aside from your writing style, there are also your moving emotions.

Han Han: In writing fiction you have the feeling that you're creating a world, one that closes up once you finish and come back to reality. And then, after a long while, if you return to take another look at that world, it's a different sort of feeling, and if you start writing again, you're not necessarily going to come up with the same good stories or emotional impact.

BYW: You are very productive, and you seem to be increasingly satisfied with your own work. How do you recharge? And a harder question: How did you escape the influence of Qian Zhongshu?

Han Han: I read books and magazines. I used to read novels before 2005 but not so much afterward. What you bring up is indeed a problem: If a book isn't a good read, it's a waste of time. If it's good, then it's hard to stop yourself from imitating it. I don't want traces of anyone else in my work, so now I only read newspapers and magazines, and I read other people's literary work as little as possible. All these years on, I'm someone who other people can imitate.

BYW: You write thundering essays in addition to your fiction, and people say that in time Han Han will be a second Lu Xun.

Han Han: I don't like Lu Xun. I don't like his literary style. He's too argumentative, and I don't like people who write too much of that. Conversely, I prefer the enemies and opponents of Lu Xun's arguments, like Liang Shiqiu, Lin Yutang, and Hu Shih.⁶ They're more generous than he was.

BYW: As far as attitude goes, I'm reminded of an advertisement you did for Nescafé: "The happiest thing about writing is when your work becomes a light for your readers. So long as you dare, there will always be a light to lead you."

Han Han: "Live boldly" might be another fitting catchphrase. Not having any regrets can be a regret. You'll discover after you've done lots of things that you were stupid or bound to fail, but you went and did them all the same. Ever since leaving school, I've done so many things, and failed so many times, so I think I rate as fairly brave and bold. Of course, you don't know about the failures, since I don't mention them. I only tell everyone about my successes. But without them I wouldn't be here today.

---

⁶ Liang Shiqiu (1903–1987), a writer, translator, and critic, is best known for his pithy essays. Lin Yutang (1895–1976) is known for his graceful style and advocacy of the importance of humor in writing. Hu Shih (1891–1962) was a leading intellectual in the May Fourth Movement and an advocate of language reform. All clashed with Lu Xun over the need for literature to be political.

THERE WILL ALWAYS BE A POWER
January 2013

> *The newspaper* Southern Weekly, *owned by the respected Southern Media Group, has been around since the 1980s and is renowned for its audacity in covering tough, sensitive topics. The paper's willingness to push boundaries has gotten it into trouble from time to time. One of the paper's traditions is a New Year's editorial expressing its vision for the coming year. Under tightening press supervision in January 2013, it was forced to run a New Year's editorial full of platitudes drafted by the party secretary instead of a bold call for better implementation of the Chinese constitution.*

When I was still an adolescent, I was deeply influenced by *Southern Weekly*, and the newspaper was my companion all those years. In the course of my writing career, and in the magazine I edited, I've been acutely aware of the meaning of their 1999 New Year editorial, "There Will Always Be a Power That Will Make Us Weep." I know, too, that a power exists that causes us not to know which course to take. The power doesn't care about what you say, what you write, or what you do. The restrictions of that power are felt throughout journalism and the arts, yet we can't see the ones who wield it. Communicating with them is even more impossible, and sometimes when you demand to know the reason, so you can "die" transparently, they'll put a hand over your mouth and tell everybody else that you're actually very happy.

You can have your so-called freedoms because they have the freedom to punish you. Whether it's literature, the news, or films and television, you have to expend a great deal of energy to get their permission. Even if you want to talk about regulations, they'll never tell you clearly what they are, which turns everyone, to a greater or lesser extent, into a rule breaker. To follow their rules, you need to become one of them. We censor ourselves and each other, often shaking with fear and trepidation, trying to figure it out. It holds on to your clothes, chokes your neck, all the while telling you to run faster and sing better so the ones who wield it will look better to the world.

We have practically no world-class authors, directors, newspapers, magazines, films. . . . Of course, you could say that these artists aren't working hard enough and are shirking their responsibility. You could say, what belongs to the nation also belongs to the world. You could ask why we should cater to other people's aesthetics. You could say Iran is a lot stricter than us, and it gave birth to ——. You could even say all the world's children enjoy our pandas. Maybe it's just me, but at least I'm not willing to have someone indiscriminately delete or edit me, tie me up and restrain me. Today's appeals aren't just for a newspaper we love and reporters and editors we respect. They're also for media outlets and media professionals who've been in much worse situations and met much worse fates. And, of course, for ourselves, too.

The *Southern Weekly* has taught me much as a reader. It has given power to the powerless and a future to pessimists, so at a time when the newspaper itself is powerless and pessimistic, may our insignificant power accompany it on its way forward.

PENNIES FOR THE WRITERS
November 2007

When it comes to charts, the table for writers' royalties is a fairly easy one to make. A writer of books doesn't engage in many commercial activities, so it's just basic arithmetic: X royalties times X sales. It's hard to count sales, of course, since journalists don't know the figures; writers might not, either; and—in the unluckiest of circumstances—the publishing house doesn't even have a clue. The only people who know are the printers. This was the case with my novel *Chaos in Chang'an*. The most reliable way to calculate how much a writer makes is by checking at the tax bureau, because tax is taken out of a writer's income. Take me, for example: I get 14 to 15 percent in royalties, or just over 12 percent after tax. These are honest numbers. So I suggest that the tax bureau produce the next writers' royalties table. In the future, if some publishing house claims that they sold more than a million copies, then please also make public the writer's royalties before and after taxes. It's a harmonious society, so bragging should be taxed, too.

This year I had an income of 3.8 million yuan. I make my money legitimately, so there is no need for tongues to wag. In general, someone with a personality like cultural critic Yu Qiuyu will remark "Too high" for any figure. But most writers don't know how much they've made: "It's really that much? I've never done the numbers."

Writers deal primarily with their emotions. They don't even know how much they make.

The figure of 3.8 million is a little large for me. This year I published only one book: *The Glorious Day*. I received over 1.9 million yuan in royalties, or 1.6 million yuan after tax. Sales of previous books bring in several hundred thousand yuan, which makes a total of about two million yuan after tax. Looks like I'll have the honor of filing a return. Last year I wasn't even qualified to file, I'm ashamed to say. The reason for that is, simply, tax from my paltry racing income didn't have to be declared, and my previous novel, *The Ideal City*, was published the year before last.

When I don't make money from racing, I supplement my income by publishing books. Cars aren't a game for me: I'm a professional racer. If cars are a game, you've got to spend money. You can give me a Mercedes-Benz, or a BMW, or a Porsche, but you'll have to pay me to drive it fast. So, based on my win at this year's championship, I'll receive an income that's about 10 percent of my royalties. Now, one friendly reminder: The best racer in the country, in the best year, will earn a salary of no more than one million yuan, for which he will risk his life racing rally and track. If you want to get rich, I'd suggest not choosing this profession.

The published rankings show that today's writers are winning on quantity and are becoming more industrialized. I heard that in the space of one year Guo Jingming, the top earner and a member of the Chinese Writers Association, published fourteen titles, a number that includes both his novels and his literary magazines. He earned three million yuan from his writing and eight million yuan from editing, which demonstrates how his talents are put to use. Of course, if you subtract from that 11 million yuan the cost of running his company, you're not left with much, since the boss pays a huge sum for a view of the Huangpu River to remind himself that he's really in Shanghai. The people he employs are all really poor, but the old saying goes, "Hire the poor writers," so they're safe on that front. Still, the rich man's team does seem particularly destitute, and poverty often changes minds.

The complete works of China's foremost children's author, Zheng Yuanjie, run to nearly fifty volumes. Scholar Yu Dan has written five or six books, and Rao Xueman (let me congratulate her here, since she published my first story in *Kids Literature*) has also written quite a few titles. We don't have the best culture for reading, and overall I don't think cranking out a lot of books every year is a long-term plan for any writer. But in recent years it's still been possible to get rich from writing, perhaps even for the composer of this list. I advise him to interview the people on it and turn it into a book called *Writers on Fortune* or *Authors Aglow*, and if it turns into a best seller, maybe next year he'll be number one. Wouldn't that be interesting! Number one on next year's list, a work that teaches you how to get to the top of the list. A world-class demonstration of teaching by example.

Looking at the numbers on the list, Chinese writers don't really earn all that much. In a population of more than one billion, how is it so difficult to produce a best seller? I truly hope that one day the best-selling book in China may earn 10 million yuan, or over a million U.S. dollars, but that wouldn't put us on par with global levels. In China we like to blow our own trumpets and say over and over again that we're a "great cultural nation," so why is it that the people of this nation don't like to read? Or how come they only like to read pirated books? Don't tell me that the real editions are too expensive. In all fairness, books are cheap products in this country. Pork

ON WEIBO AND WECHAT
February 2013

Weibo, a social media platform run by Sina, one of China's leading Internet portals, offers functionality somewhere between Twitter and Facebook. The rise of WeChat, similar to WhatsApp—a social media app for mobile devices developed by Tencent, another Internet giant—eclipsed Weibo, just as Weibo took the place of earlier platforms in China's social media landscape.

I received the following question from readers: "Less than a year ago you created a Weibo account, and a while back you topped 10 million followers. How do you feel about that?" At the same time I was asked, "Do you use WeChat, what do you think of it, and what's your ID?" Apart from "What's your ID?" my answers are as follows:

In my personal opinion, by taking the number of your followers on Weibo too seriously, you're hypnotizing and deceiving yourself. I can't speak for anyone else, but for me, at least, I've definitely got quite a few zombie fans, weird fans, and inactive fans. The number is clearly inflated. I don't care if saying that makes me look bad. In the real world, why would so many people truly want to friend me? But if you're willing and the Web site allows it, your follower count can go however high you want.

Weibo has its advantages, of course. News is no longer so easily blocked, speech is freer, and at certain exceptional moments it's the only thing left. But at the same time, everything's a mirage. If something you write or a joke you retell gets reposted tens of thousands of times, you feel like your famous sentences are being passed around in the streets, like it's some sort of event that people are compelled to get involved in and that everyone, including the cactuses in the Taklamakan Desert, is talking about it.

My feeling is that if you indulge, what you're getting, apart from a bit of inspiration and the same information you could obtain elsewhere, is pure emotion. You want to maintain your objectivity and cool, but you end up spending too much time trying to judge if the information is real or fake. You refresh the page again and again, and think you've learned quite a lot through gossip mills large and small, but the next day you've forgotten it entirely. No, it's more stirring to have a long chat with a friend, a meal with the family, or— for me—an outing with my daughter. Weibo actually has an ecology similar to Chinese society: One in a thousand, a tenth of 1 percent, have status and a voice, four in a thousand are working hard for themselves, and 999 are commoners, just blades of grass. When the wind kicks up over sandy ground, optimistic grasses think they're the wind, pessimists think they're the sand. And the other five? They're pretending to be the tenth of 1 percent.

Nowadays I tend to use WeChat quite a bit more than Weibo. My "friendship circle" is growing rowdier by the day, and at least for the people around me who fall into the 999, friendship circles convince them they exist. What they post gets seen by the people who ought to, unlike Weibo posts that go un-reposted, uncommented on, and totally overlooked or ignored. A blade of grass on Weibo that has no intention of getting famous can be right about a thousand things, but quite often no one even sees what you've posted, but if you're not careful and say the wrong thing, you might be dragged out and paraded in the streets. The time may come when what you've posted on Weibo will get you into trouble. At least in a friendship circle you can do what you want. On Weibo, you often have to perform as a better version of yourself, someone closer to what others need you to be. Still, as I see quotes from author Wang Shuo, CCTV's Bai Yansong, Alibaba's Jack Ma, and mob boss Du Yuesheng, and even myself crop up more and more often in my WeChat friendship circle, it can get annoying. When I see a good friend suddenly "Like" something I supposedly said but would never actually say as much, my emotions are in conflict. The same person often appears in two guises, one for Weibo and the other for WeChat. Today, for example, he might share a dog hot pot dinner on WeChat, but tomorrow he denounces eating dog meat on Weibo. I'm not plugging Tencent here. Tencent's also responsible for a lot of crap. As for other microblog systems on other Web sites, I've peeked at my accounts there, and although they've also attracted "ten million" fans, I let that go with a smile. I suspect that they have fewer active users than the population of my neighborhood. Yeah, certain Internet companies might calculate that I've already used three hundred thousand characters to answer this question. If Weibo manages to stick around, I'm really looking forward to the first "Huge V," a verified account whose number of fans exceeds the total number of Chinese Internet users and is on track to pass the population of Earth.

As a writer, it's necessary to go many places with a smartphone. I haven't done enough, nor have I gone far enough.

FOR EVERY SELF
April 2012

Shortly before the Spring Festival in 2012, Han Han was accused by a number of prominent bloggers of not being the author of the books and blog posts published under his name. His attackers postulated that he and his publishers had arranged for either his father or a team of ghostwriters to do the actual writing, with Han Han just a figurehead whose fame was harnessed to sell books and influence public opinion. The controversy highlighted procedural irregularities in the New Concept Writing Competition, which he won in 1999, and the circumstances behind the drafting of his first novel, Triple Door. *One of his chief critics was Fang Zhouzi, a well-known science writer and tenacious fraud buster, with whom Han Han traded barbs several times before eventually bowing out of the fight with the following post.*

The last three months I've experienced every aspect of humanity, and have come away with both sadness and reward. Sadness because I used to think my story inspirational: I was born a rural loser and started with nothing, no power or influence. Now, what was a "loser's counterattack," is actually an earth-shattering conspiracy packaged by mysterious forces. Sadness also comes from the fact that my "celebrity friend" in Beijing, who I'd met only a couple of times, bafflingly fabricated and disseminated an inside story about me. It chilled me, although out of compassion I want to believe he was just blabbing without thinking. And sadness because I care too much, I worry too much about being portrayed as doing something I didn't do, and I've started to get cautious. But I feel rewarded because I've seen loyalty from friends and strangers who were prompted to speak out for justice even though they were later condemned as an "interest group." Rewarded because I gained the support of classmates I had ten years ago, even though the differences in the stories we told when recollecting ancient memories prompted others to call us frauds. Rewarded because I've now seen the many different hearts of man, so my fictional characters will be even more wonderful.

Personalities and approaches to problems don't stay constant, especially between the ages of sixteen and thirty. I've written some good essays, and I've also written some shitty ones, but quality and stylistic changes illustrate growth, since nothing's static for fourteen years. In my early twenties I supported a boycott of Japanese goods. I was a nationalist. But in 2008, I opposed the Carrefour boycott. When I was younger I advocated war and the retaking of Taiwan, but now I'm embarrassed to even admit it. When I was seventeen or eighteen, I boasted: "Out of all the essay writers alive, I'm second best." How this makes me blush now! But I blush even harder when I remember that I thought Li Ao* was the best. Back then I pretended to be cool—I sought to shock with my words—but

---

* Li Ao, a prominent essayist and social activist in Taiwan who spent time in jail during the 1970s and '80s on political charges, is known for his sharp tongue and independent political stance.

those words now disgust me. Digging up stupid comments affects people in different ways. Who wasn't young once? Repeat today the ignorant things you said in your dorm rooms, or the immature declarations of love you made in the woods, and everyone would die laughing. No one remains identical to their past self, unless you never grow up.

Anyone who knows me knows that I'm actually shy and cautious when it comes to strangers. I've been this way since childhood. That side of my personality finds release in writing and racing. So long as I'm not kicked out, I can serve five or six years on the same car team. If I'm in collaboration with a party and there are no incidents, I'll continue with the collaboration. I always stay at the same hotels, eat at the same two or three restaurants, and order the same couple of dishes. This is who I am. Perhaps this is because I resist change and uncertainty in my life, a life that is so different from most and filled with so many uncertainties. I've never said I was especially elegant, and some people have dug out my teen and young adult television interviews, editing the bad parts together to prove I'm a hick.

I believe that every one of you seated at the computer has been blessed by the creator with a special ability; it's just that many of you haven't discovered it. Maybe right now there are lots of Mozarts programming computers, Michael Schumachers writing reports, Maggie Cheungs working at reception, and Kai-Fu Lees working as real estate agents.† I'm just

---

† Maggie Cheung (born 1964) is an award-winning Hong Kong actress best known for her starring role in Wong Kar-wai's *In the Mood for Love* (2000). Kai-Fu Lee (born 1961) was the founding president of Google China and now runs a venture capital firm focusing on IT start-ups.

luckier than a lot of people: I found something I like and that suits me. In many ways I'm dumber than you and I'll never learn. Anyone, despite their many shortcomings, still does certain things better than other people. And those are the signs that make you different. The creator is fair. It's up to you whether you discover those signs.

I STILL WANT TO BE A STINKING PUBLIC INTELLECTUAL

A decade into the new millennium, Han Han had become recognized within China as the spokesperson for his generation. As his blog posts transitioned from personal observations on life and racing to literary debates to incisive commentary on hot-button social issues—precisely what had first made him famous as a student a decade before—he and those who supported him began to gain grudging mainstream acceptance as critics whose voices could not be ignored. Han Han's appeal drew in part from his ability to thread the needle between the antigovernment rhetoric of the liberal right and the nationalism of the red left. He staked out a position based on common sense and self-deprecation (not to mention national-deprecation), all laced with his trademark satire.

But in essays and interviews, Han Han often expressed a shifting sense of discomfort with his fame, especially as his stance on social, cultural, and historical issues evolved. Recognizing the way that online communities form echo chambers as provocative opinion leaders hurl abuse at each other, he distanced himself from the dust-ups of his early blogging career and learned to behave with decorum in the public eye.

He broadened his horizons with trips to Thailand and Taiwan, returning with a more nuanced understanding of his own society, and honed his already keen sense of right and wrong. Less of a hothead, he was—to the establishment—no less a troublemaker.

I STILL WANT TO BE A STINKING PUBLIC INTELLECTUAL
March 2012

The term public *intellectual* has a stink that grows worse by the day, but it's not just in the past couple of years that the name has been maligned. I remember how lots of magazines used to pick the year's top public intellectuals—I was a candidate once—but at some point people began to use the term as an insult. There'd be two sides, both of them clearly public intellectuals, and when they were in mid-debate, one would shout, "You're a bunch of public intellectuals!" and the other side would be defeated without argument. It was a retort even more effective than accusing an attacker of driving off in a BMW. Later, people wised up and presented themselves as commoners from the start, but it wasn't long before debates between ordinary people became a lose-lose situation, a tussle between "shitizens" of interest to no one. Before long, the term *public opinion leaders* was created, and shortly afterward you had a whole flood of them online. You could watch public opinion leaders automatically assemble whenever there was a public incident, but why not watch Yi Jianlian play basketball instead? Finally, the big guns came out. *Citizen*, a word that was both safe and not easily maligned, made its entrance as a popular variant of *public intellectual*. Nevertheless, people have recently been saying that so-called citizens are just out for fame, that they're just calling attention to themselves. As a result, people don't know what to call this group.

The befouling of *public intellectual* is due in part to public intellectuals themselves. Indeed, intellectuals have a host of ugly problems: Some are pedantic, some are oily, some are lecherous, some are flaky, some are opportunistic, some are long-winded, some are crude, some are posers, some are obscurantists, some play to the crowd, some are insular, some put on airs, some have poor character, some are hypocritical, some are alarmist, and some are factionalist. And since they're always talking, their personal shortcomings are magnified until they become downright annoying. But, taking a step back, that's the case for everyone in all walks of life. It's like saying celebrity relationships are messy. Take a look around your office: Are things any better? This is probably how it went: Lots of people were initially gratified when public intellectuals and opinion leaders began holding forth, since they gave voice to their heart's concerns, although the people wondered why they were so rambling and repetitious. You can't put all the blame on public intellectuals, of course, since the bulk of the responsibility lies with a government that's forever guilty of rambling repetition. Later, someone cried out, "Public intellectuals have fame and fortune, but they're not that great. They're just consumers of politics and sentiment. Stinking public intellectuals!"

A friend of mine doesn't like to read social criticism by public intellectuals with a literary background, because he feels it's too much of a performance, and the camera never stops rolling as they flub their lines. Instead, he prefers listening to successful businesspeople. He follows the microblogs of people like Kai-Fu Lee, Wang Ran, and Pan Shiyi, and he retweets them every day. Stylistically speaking, he feels they're no worse than the literati, and the better understanding they have of what's feasible in the real world makes them much more pleasant to read. Most importantly, they're already wealthy and have no need to perform. "Not necessarily," said another friend at a dinner a little while later. He advanced a conspiracy theory: "When you're rich, you need a good reputation, so I question their motives. It's just another form of consumption, and they're another type of stinking public intellectual." My first friend contested this, but the next day he retweeted nothing but lame jokes, and it took him a few more days to recover.

Another friend of mine likes the actress Yao Chen because she's one of the few celebrities to speak out in a show-biz world disconnected from reality. Other friends are dismissive and say that it might all be part of a plan to set her apart from other celebrities—which, when you get right down to it, benefits her. Just another variant of stinking public intellectual.

I've got another friend who likes ————* and thinks he's really awesome. A different friend countered that he's just adopting a pose, and that the more he's persecuted, the higher he's rated and the more money he makes. He's operating on a higher plane than the stinking public intellectuals, but he, too, is consuming politics. In a nutshell: Stinking Public Intellectual version 2.0.

So now I get to myself. In my junior high essays I used to love tossing criticism around, but I had no overall concept

---

* This probably refers to the contemporary artist Ai Weiwei, whose name is blocked as a "sensitive word" on many social media platforms due to his social activism and vocal criticism of the government.

beyond the fact that reading authors from the Republican period during my formative years gave me the subconscious feeling that writing ought to be critical. A classmate of mine was mad about writing, too, but our reading material and personalities were totally different. I can understand why some people are concerned with the world while others care about astrology, and there's nothing wrong with any of that. My first book may have been a best seller, but my inflated reputation is due to the opinion pieces I've written over the past few years. Since I live well and am still able to publish, there's suspicion that I'm a paid plant, a "Fifty-Center,"[†] or a troll. A Stinking Public Intellectual 3.0.

In this latest round, I've encountered the attitude that if you're reasonably well-off, or at least not dead in the streets, you'll be subjected to all kinds of wild speculation. If you're the least bit radical, that's posturing. A little conservative, and you're a government stooge. Either way you're consuming politics and public events. Whenever public intellectuals' viewpoints differ even the slightest bit, they tend to go at each other with a vengeance, leaving the public with the impression that they're all a bunch of bastards. For that reason, and because of the increasingly powerful pen of the general public, *public intellectual* has gone from a term of praise to a means of manipulating the truth.

And so I've finally come to the understanding that, regardless of whether I affirm or deny it or if I come up with a

---

[†] This derogatory name comes from the widespread belief that some segment of the Internet population is paid 0.5 yuan per comment they post in support of certain positions, typically in favor of the government.

substitute term for myself, I'm still a stinking public intellectual. Who, you may ask, cares about the name of the group? Call them intellectuals, public intellectuals, opinion leaders, or citizens; so long as you speak for yourself, your reputation is your own, and it doesn't matter at all whether those terms are fragrant or foul. But it still feels wrong to me. Say you're as unattached as a wild stork drifting among the clouds. You're not going to want your group to be suddenly stigmatized as you're flying along, and to have people point at you and say, "Look, there goes a wild duck." Of course, much of that might stem from the fact that the wild storks are all accusing each other of being wild ducks while a bunch of cocks watch on from the sidelines. The wild pigs in charge of everything love seeing how the terminology changes. For me, *intellectual* and *public intellectual* ought to be positive words to be treasured no matter the era, meaning that the very title of this essay is an offense. Not so much for *opinion leader*. Anything with *leader* in it ends up cutting off all divergent directions.

Yes, I am an intellectual. I consume politics, I consume current events, and I consume hot-button issues. I consume the vested interests of public power. You all are able to consume me, too, and you don't even need to leave a tip. Wouldn't it be better if everyone could safely consume public authority and politics? Wouldn't it be great if everyone was concerned about the world, criticized social injustice, condemned heinous deeds when they are revealed, and celebrated when corrupt officials are taken in? So what if it's just posturing or a trick to get fans, women, and praise? When faced with government, public power, and politics, if you don't consume them, they will likely destroy you.

Ultimately, before all manner of injustice, no one can consume for you. You've got to do it yourself. Popular

OFFICIALS AND ME
April 2012

Some time ago an official used the Weibo microblog platform as if it were actually QQ instant messaging software, and now yesterday someone who apparently is a civil servant used Weibo as his personal notebook to write down lots of titillating yet commonplace stories about officialdom. We can't draw any conclusions as to whether it was an artistic work or a muddleheaded diary. I have raced throughout the country and can't avoid coming into contact with officials, and I have mixed feelings toward them. I've had some weird conversations over the years, and today I'm going to get them off my chest. I've concealed the time and place, so you might as well read this as if it's fiction.

1. In 2008, the head of a Shanghai district found me through a series of friends and acquaintances, and called me up to ask if I could help him, since his district was planning to host a talk by a famous writer. They had a certain budget, in the tens of thousands of yuan. "I'm not suitable," I said. He replied, "Oh, you've misunderstood. We just wanted you to act as a go-between for us with Yu Qiuyu, the cultural critic. You're both writers, so you must know each other."

2. In 200X, at a rally race in a prefectural-level city in the south, the government organized a welcome banquet

for the participants, in which I was forced by the race committee to take part. Because I was moderately famous, I was seated at the main table. I sat down in a random seat at a dinner table roughly the same size as the center circle on a soccer field, and thought gloomily that if a dish were to be set in the middle, I'd have to climb out of my seat to reach it with my chopsticks. I didn't know if I was supposed to let the leaders climb out of their seats first. Feeling moody as I looked around, I noticed that all the officials at the table were looking at me strangely and seemed about to say something. We stared at one another, and then an awkward-looking person resembling a typical secretary came over and said into my ear, "Mr. Driver Han Han, I'm really sorry, but you're sitting in the mayor's seat."

3. After the mayor sat down, we chitchatted a bit and then all of a sudden he said loudly: "I heard you're a writer. I hope you'll help us promote the city of S———. Urban construction and spiritual civilization have been developing quickly the last few years." Immediately, someone added, "Yes, yes, yes, and especially after the mayor took his post." I said, "The most impressive construction is this hotel and your offices. Why don't I write an essay praising them?" As soon as the words left my mouth I knew they were impolite, but unexpectedly everyone at the table agreed that it was a great idea.

4. A press conference was held before a race at a certain place. A local civil servant picked me up to go to the conference center. "Your government has some really beautiful trees," I said. He replied, proudly, "Of course. This one's valued at . . ."

5. In 2010, I presented a lecture. The officials who invited me—open-minded, decent people who liked art—also invited a few other friends who I rather admired for daring to express their anger. I walked onstage and said: "My talk today is 'Better City, Worse Life.'"* After my talk, I called a friend who was watching the online broadcast and asked how it went. My friend said, "I only heard the first line, and then it cut to commercials, and then you never reappeared." But, to be fair, in the city of Shanghai—apart from high-stressed living and tight controls on culture—public safety and the environment are fairly good by Chinese standards.

6. During a race at a certain county in the north, the team arranged for me to eat with local officials. At a toast from the table next to us, my teammate tried to beg off by saying he had to race later and it would be bad if he was caught drinking and driving. The official said: "Don't worry, that's not a problem. The guy making the toast is on the traffic police corps. When you've eaten, how about we organize a sauna for you to relax before the race? Don't feel awkward. Come, I'll ask our security team leader. He knows just the place."

7. The secretary to the head of county G—— contacted me through the e-mail address on my blog to say that the county leader also happened to be an entrepreneur. He would be happy to pay me a high price if I'd

---

* The slogan of the 2010 Shanghai Expo was "Better City, Better Life."

help write his biography and tell the world about his glorious political record.

8. A high official of a certain prefectural-level city in the southwest contacted me through a sports reporter on the racing circuit to ask me to write a book for him. He also mentioned his experiences and what he's learned from building an intellectual and ideological civilization. His condition was that we halve the royalties.

9. My friend Z, who works in the culture industry, once applied to a fund for supporting the arts and asked me for a signed copy of my book to give to the person responsible for approving the application. But he was rejected. I'd seen his application plan, which was quite well written, and I couldn't for the life of me understand why it was denied. Later a friend said to me, "You morons. You really gave him just a book? You didn't put anything inside?"

10. A friend's father is the mayor of a certain town. The default homepage on his office computer is their local government Web site, which has a bunch of links at the bottom leading to different functional departments, like the Economic and Trade Commission, the Science and Technology Commission, and the Civil Affairs Bureau. So for months he wandered around official Web sites that had never been updated, gaining an impression that the Internet wasn't as bad an influence on officials as the outside world made it out to be. Then one day someone pointed him to a Web portal. . . . So when I read that an official had been using Weibo as if it were QQ, I wasn't surprised at all.

11. I once read a news article reporting that after a mayor of a certain city was bitten by a dog, he issued an order for all dogs in the city to be killed. As a dog lover, I raged at the absurdity of this and immediately reposted it to my blog. Two years later I received a phone call out of the blue from the public security department of God-knows-where demanding that I delete a post from a certain year, month, and day. I asked which post it was, and they said righteously, with perfectly correct enunciation, "It's the post 'Comrade ———— Was Bitten by a Dog.'" "Is it because the mayor who was bitten by a dog got a promotion?" I asked. The other end went quiet. "I really don't care about deleting it," I said. "I'm just annoyed that you dispatched your police so slowly."

These are the only anecdotes I have for the time being, and I worry as I write them down whether I'm being honest and kind enough. But on reconsideration, though officialdom may be unshakable, officials themselves have a high rate of turnover. What I've described happened years ago, and no one knows where those officials are now: promoted, demoted, or crashed like a North Korean rocket? It's their game, and they have their own rules for living. Some are magnificent and soul stirring; others never make the right move and lose their wits. As for the rest of us, we give our support to the good, ignore the bad, and laugh at the stupid, waiting for the time when they finally self-destruct. That's all we can do.

AN AMERICAN SOAP OPERA IN CHONGQING
February 2012

> *Wang Lijun was the vice mayor of Chongqing and the head of the city's public security bureau. Demoted during a corruption investigation on February 2, he visited the U.S. consulate in the neighboring city of Chengdu on February 6, remaining for around twenty-four hours before leaving voluntarily, whereupon he was detained by state security personnel. His consular visit, the subject of which remains secret, set in motion the downfall of Chongqing party secretary Bo Xilai. This post was made while Wang was in detention, which Chongqing authorities described as "vacation-style medical treatment."*

Last night, I believe that many netizens, just like me, were madly refreshing the People Online Web site. I'd guess that this must be the first time that People Online has welcomed so many real "people." All that refreshing was for only two words: Wang Lijun.

Who'd have thought Wang Lijun would turn out to be a central character, ending up at the U.S. consulate and producing an American soap opera? A domestic soap you starred in feels like playacting by comparison.

This brought to mind my rally races years ago that were

held in county towns. Because I was a seeded racer, it was always a county official who called the car for me; but the next year, although the announcer read the same titles, the people who appeared had different faces. After the cars were called, I followed the announcer's line, "Will the leaders leave the stage?" and stared at the retreating figures of the leaders, a million thoughts in my mind. Some of them had been promoted, of course, while others had been axed. What specifically happened in Chongqing, in the center of this political gossip mill, we'll never see clearly. News in the mainland is opaque, People Online isn't humane, and I was only able to follow the trail of rumors and scrape together a rough picture. In the process, I entered the heart of Comrade Wang Lijun and picked out one word: *exhaustion*.

Chinese officials have identities that are split to an extreme. In the mornings they enter the meeting room, and in the evenings they enter the club; in one respect they have to study and understand '60s-style documents; in another they have to carefully differentiate between QQ and Weibo; as they criticize America, they also have to know where precisely the U.S. consulate is. "Here, you won't understand China," to twist a slogan. I sincerely feel their pain. I've just followed a Chongqing-flavored American soap for an evening, with a plot that's up and down, full of twists and turns, the news arriving thick and fast. If I feel like I need a holiday to recuperate, what about the central character, Wang Lijun? I guess he must be in shock.

So I don't understand what Chinese officials are thinking. Lots of people want to become officials—that's a given, and especially a prominent official—since, if you want to do business, you don't need to do fund-raising the same way as

entrepreneur Wu Ying,* who bought hers with the death penalty. All you need to do is arrange for a relative to monopolize
a particular resource, and then telephone the bank. When
an official gains enough seniority, the ups and downs aren't
something that ordinary people like us can understand. An
official who had to resign after the 2010 Shanghai fire was
quite quickly able to get a post in Xinjiang. (Good thing he
wasn't assigned to Karamay.)† Those who manipulate public opinion organs today will be negative news tomorrow;
those who operate the machine of state today will tomorrow
be carried off by that very machine. Rather than describing
officials as "corrupt" or "honest," people use *on the rise* or *in
decline*. And yet no one knows what will happen in Chongqing, even though that city just led the singing of red songs
in Hong Kong, a city where previously the only "Red" they'd
heard sung was the song by pop star Leslie Cheung.

The cloak-and-dagger nature of this event tells me that
in the future, we don't need to predict a color. Red or blue,
they'll never beat transparent.

---

* Wu Ying (born 1981) was a Zhejiang businesswoman and was for-
merly the sixth richest woman in China. Her arrest in 2009 for illegal fund-raising and subsequent death penalty sentence sparked a
debate on the propriety of capital punishment for economic crimes,
which include common strategies private businesses resort to when
banks are reluctant to extend loans. Wu's death sentence was reduced in 2012 and commuted in 2014.

† Karamay, Xinjiang, was the site of a tragic fire on December 8, 1994,
that killed 324 people, 288 of them schoolchildren. In popular accounts of the catastrophe, students were supposedly told to let the
leaders exit first.

SOME PEOPLE SHOULD GET THE VOTE FIRST
February 2012

First of all, this essay was meant to be called "Flowers of the Opposite Shore." I was halfway through writing it before the Spring Festival, before the fabulous discussion we were having got interrupted.* I found the discussion immensely beneficial, and after reading lots of essays, I'd like to adjust some of my previous viewpoints. They're still under warranty, though, so I'll hold off a bit on making the adjustments. By the time the flowers bloom in spring, I look forward to "speaking again of revolution," "pressing again for freedom," and "speaking again about democracy." It surprised me that these dry topics were of interest to anyone, since when I inquired of my young friends, they told me that, out of everything I've written, they like to read my . . . film reviews. I've even seen the following aphorism: "China is a Mao-Deng society. Hua couldn't solve it, Hu messed around for a few years, Zhao was useless, too, Jiang made do, Hu messed around again,

---

* At the end of December 2011, Han Han posted three essays, "Speaking of Revolution," "Pressing for Revolution," and "Speaking About Democracy," whose explicitly political content proved controversial, with some critics feeling that he was overly sympathetic to the establishment. All three can be found in English in *This Generation*.

so Xi feels completely normal."[†] There's lots of information here, but at the same time it expresses that all that you care about is useless, and if you're not careful you'll get yourself in trouble.

When you're married, you find that if you care about the future of the country, you're actually caring about yourself. Everyone, to a greater or lesser or deeper or lighter extent, wants to discuss this or even act to change society. Meanwhile, Taiwan has held elections. There may be many intrinsic differences between Taiwan and the mainland, but neither Chiang Kai-shek nor Mao Zedong could have predicted that the Nationalist counterattack on the mainland would be like this, without soldiers or weapons. This set me to looking back at my own history, to the first time I experienced an election.

When I was still in primary school, the class elected a class president. I think there were forty-two people in our class, and each classmate could vote for more than one person. Because I was loved by all, and my grades were extraordinary (I was on the student committee in elementary school: Don't be shocked, every fatty was skinny once), I got the full forty-two votes. My opponent had one vote fewer. Regrettably, in the end I didn't get to be class president because the teacher said: "You aren't modest at all. You can't get all the votes. How could you vote for yourself?"

[†] This quotation from some anonymous Internet user is brimming with wordplay on the surnames of China's leaders since Mao Zedong (Deng Xiaoping, Hua Guofeng, Hu Yaobang, Zhao Ziyang, Jiang Zemin, Hu Jintao, and Xi Jinping). *Mao-Deng* is meant to echo the English word *modern*, but the remainder are homophones for Chinese words.

And so I was out of the election. Even though I am now opposed to student cadre elections, that tally on the blackboard remains deeply etched in my mind. I have never looked at another ballot. It's been over twenty years since opening up and reform began, and everyone remembers what Deng Xiaoping said in 1985: "Let some people get rich first," a statement that turned into an unofficial slogan. There's no question now that the slogan has become reality. It's even exceeded its quota. Some people are filthy fucking rich, and ordinary people seem even poorer by contrast even though the middle class is growing. Economic reforms have been going on for years, so let's set aside the question of failure and success for the moment; there's still been no improvement in political reforms. See how the Eighteenth National Congress of the Communist Party hasn't even been held yet, and the people already think Xi Jinping's completely normal!

To tell you the truth, I don't know if it's realistic to expect Chinese people to vote for a president using one person, one vote, since social classes differ too much in size and are splitting apart, and regional development is unbalanced. It seems like only a despot or dictator, rather than democracy or reforms, can finish everything at once to complete the journey. I can actually accept knowing now who will be president in 2012 and who will be premier, just like there was no problem with Deng Xiaoping's appointed successor. But many young friends around me (I'm talking about friends I know, not in the abstract, who through discussion of democracy and reform have granted me the right to represent them) seriously hope that another slogan can be added to the reform and opening up: "Let some people get the vote first."

As for what people and in which regions, none of that matters. What's really important is to know what they're voting for. Administrative voting began in villages in China a long time ago, but this is too small of a step. Political power has been established for nearly a century, so we should at least be voting for our mayors now. Of course, I don't even care if at the start the candidates are chosen by the people or if they're officially selected. It doesn't matter. For example, in the city of Shanghai, there could be at least three candidates for mayor nominated by those in power, and then let them freely debate on television and in the newspapers and propose their plans. Then let them go to the districts and counties and make public speeches. To rig an election at village level is very easy (it's better to have a rigged election than no election at all), but it's much harder to rig an election at a municipal level. When open mayoral elections are going on in some big city, people all over the country should watch closely and have mock elections in order to foster involvement and prepare for actual engagement. At the same time, new mayors should be elected every three years, and People's Congress delegates should be able to get together and impeach the mayor, giving them an actual purpose at last. If we elect mayors one by one, there'll no longer be a need for the much-maligned petitions system.‡ I seriously believe that as long as mayors are elected, even if they remain Party members for the time being, they'll still

---

‡ Under China's petition system, citizens can submit grievances to the State Bureau for Letters and Calls, which then routes them through proper government channels for resolution. Before the rules were reformed in late 2013, local officials were evaluated based on the number of petitioners in their jurisdiction, motivating them to organize the interception and detention of petitioners before they could submit their complaints to the capital.

have some qualms where the people are concerned, whereas now they care only about currying favor with their superiors. If they break the law, all that would happen would be that the people could get rid of them, since they're clearly incompetent. They wouldn't have to hide in the U.S. embassy, afraid for their lives. For an official, this is a release. For the people of the country, it's the most lively exercise of democracy.

We shouldn't rely on the Propaganda Department for a stable society but should take a few steps forward.

I wanted to join the volunteers' army for a second War to Resist U.S. Aggression and Aid Korea. And when I was in junior high, I was in favor of taking back Taiwan by military force. In my most ignorant moment, I imagined that a dog chain I picked up was the Nebula Chain from the anime Saint Seiya. No individual's opinion of the world will remain unchanged. Even if Ma Nan didn't change her opinion, there's still no logical moral relationship between challenging Clinton and marrying an American. Never mind that I checked up on the news a few years ago and found out that Ma Nan never studied in the U.S. or obtained a Green Card: It was pure rumor.

As for Liu Yiting, *Triple Door* was published at the time that the book *Harvard Girl Liu Yiting* was really popular. She's had an outstanding life in the U.S. Every person follows their own road; I tread my wild path, she walks on her highway. Both paths are worth following as long as they are not twisted or evil. Every path can lead to success. The same goes for Huang Silu. We were in touch after the CCTV program, and we exchanged best wishes. From what I know, she's now also very successful and is living a happy life. Success doesn't just mean fame. If you're established or outstanding in your own field, or if you have a loving family life, then you're already successful. Fame in this age is crap anyway, since all the idiots who push the limits of propriety have fans gathered around their knees. Can anyone *not* have a voice when they're watching their Weibo updates, guesting on television shows as a tongue-clicking bootlicker and punching bag, pretending to be famous? But is that really a voice? Huang Silu, Liu Yiting, and Ma Nan chose with their hearts. I know similar rumors are liable to incite racial tensions. Although the whole mess of unverified and unconnected information may be advantageous to me, it damages people's reputations. Discontent with current social ills shouldn't be married to three girls who haven't done anything wrong. They are independent, they studied abroad, they fell in love with foreigners, and all of this is good. I stayed in China, I didn't marry a foreign chick, but that doesn't make me noble.

I really haven't given any thought to emigrating. Not for any lofty reason, and I'm not afraid you'll spin a conspiracy theory about my motivations. If we're being honest, I wouldn't be able to adjust to life abroad. My friends, my family, my relatives, my readers, my racing team, and my races—they're all here. I like reading Chinese characters and eating Chinese food. The reason I love the land is because of the people standing on it. I will be where my loved ones are. There's another reason, of course, one I mentioned when I answered a Canadian journalist's question a few years ago: "In China, I'm surrounded by corrupt officials. I'm already used to it. If I go to another country and discover I'm still surrounded by corrupt Chinese officials, I'd go completely mad."

Lastly, I want to give my best wishes to any friends who have emigrated, to those residing abroad, and to those students who studied abroad and never returned. I hope you will breathe for me a couple more gasps of that free and clean air, and I hope that you may create new things in a more just environment. What has benefited you will sooner or later benefit us.

SLAUGHTER THE PUBLIC

From Beijing Youth Weekly
July 2012

On Public Intellectuals

BYW: If there are too many voices, a flood of opinions, then won't public intellectuals, or so-called opinion leaders, just be the leading complainers?

Han Han: That's what they already are. But complaining is one means of social progress.

BYW: You once issued a very showy declaration in an early 2012 blog post: "A good writer who slaughters the powerful should also slaughter the public."* Why did you choose to use the inflammatory term *slaughter*?

Han Han: I couldn't find another word. I couldn't use *massacre*, and I couldn't use *criticize*, since that's too banal, so I chose *slaughter*.

---

* To highlight distinctions in vocabulary, this is a more literal rendering of a line from the blog post "This Last Year of Mine" that was translated in *This Generation* as "A good writer shouldn't just train his sights on the high and mighty; he should also be ready to clip the wings of the masses" (p. 252).

BYW: Don't you think many people feel that by criticizing the powerful and showing compassion to the people, or even currying favor with them, you're making the clear statement that "along the road to democracy, the greatest obstacle is the people?"[†]

Han Han: One of the obstacles. Of the two sides, you ought to criticize the powerful first, for the simple reason that when the powerful are chasing profit, the ordinary people are the ones to suffer. But this doesn't mean that a good writer ought to endlessly attempt to please the people. My point is, so what? I'm not trying to please anyone. After writing for so many years, I know that pleasing people isn't easy.

BYW: That "So what?" attitude really seems like you.

Han Han: When you get down to it, I slant a little bit right. But I don't have much of a connection to the rest of the right wing. My friends are mostly my childhood playmates and high school classmates, and our relationship is based on football and fishing. None of them have any interest in my writing. We care about living, not arguments.

---

† From an April 14, 2008, blog post.

REMEMBERING A TIME WHEN I WAS POWERLESS
October 2008

Last night, when I was riding my motorbike on the Shenzhuan Highway in Shanghai, I saw something strange on the ground. I swerved to avoid it—it looked like a sea of rocks—and had to go into the oncoming lane. The stones, of all sizes, were spread a distance of several dozen meters, and whoever drove over them would end up with at best a flat tire and busted rim; a little worse, damaged parts on the undercarriage; and worse yet, a traffic accident. The worst case of all would be if a biker didn't notice it at all. I understood why the government wants to ban motorbikes: They're thinking of the people. Chinese roads are extremely dangerous and are not yet suitable for motorcycle traffic.

Obviously, the rocks had fallen off a seriously overloaded truck. It's hard for me to understand why the government hassles cars and motorbikes in the name of environmental protection but is incredibly lenient toward trucks. I'll venture to say that our car exhaust is very environmentally friendly, since the cars we buy satisfy the government's latest strict environmental standards and we only use fuel that the government monopoly says is good. However, the exhaust and emissions from many of our trucks, buses, and factories are substandard. But let's set that aside for now.

Four or five cars were parked at the emergency exit,

probably all from punctured tires. Some of the cars wouldn't be leaving anytime soon, since they had two or three busted tires but only one spare. They may have been victims, but I don't understand why one of them didn't take a caution sign, something they all possessed, and set it up fifty meters ahead of the rocks to prevent misfortune for all the cars that followed. I understand, of course, how a victim feels helpless, and although I bear malice toward none, if I were a victim, I'd still feel better the more people I had there with me.

So I started thinking inside my helmet of all the things I could do. It was easy to come up with lots of things, but after a little thought, I realized that nothing would help.

My first idea was to ask for a caution sign from one of the victims, but I decided against it. The people suffering from flats on the roadside were the masses ignorant of the truth, angry and emotionally unstable, so clearly this would be an inappropriate action.

I could ride my motorbike back to the rocks on the road and park in front as a warning, but I decided against that, because people who couldn't see the rocks wouldn't see a motorbike. If they crashed into my motorbike, it would cause serious damage to both parties, and I'd have to pay compensation. In China, it's common to get screwed when you do something good. So this obviously wasn't the right tactic.

I could ride back to the intersection, pull up even with a car, and then tap on their window and point out the area of foreign objects in front of them. But I decided against it because they'd almost certainly think I was part of a "flying bike squad" of purse snatchers. If they panicked and hit me, or if they rightfully defended themselves, I'd be dead. And even if they were naïve enough to think I was a madman rather than a purse snatcher, their attention would still be focused on me. They'd smack into the rocks, for sure.

Or I could get off my bike and go move the rocks, but I decided against it, because they covered a vast area and I'd have to work for five hours straight. And if someone thought I was actually scattering them rather than picking them up, I'd be done for. Besides, doing something like that is an affectation in China today, and if someone recognized me, I'd be even worse off. It would turn into something planned, a conspiracy, a show that I'd put on.

I could stand on the road directing traffic and wait for the police to come, but I decided against it. I was riding a motorbike, which meant I was a lawbreaker and a criminal, since the motorbike—a mode of transport recognized the world over—isn't recognized in our country, except, of course, for the BMWs that cost 300,000 yuan and are used by police or serve as official escorts. No other high-displacement motorbikes are allowed on the road. I'd direct traffic for ages, and in the end the police would come and take away my motorbike. What an effect that would have on my worldview. I guess that's how you get people who snap like Ma Jiajue.* I'm actually a good person, yet the world sees me as bad.

Or, since I couldn't just do nothing, I'd call the police. I dialed 110 but I was told, "Our system is busy. Please call back later." Luckily I hadn't taken a spill and was calling for help before I slipped into a coma. If heaven only granted me one

---

* In 2004, Ma Jiajue, a student at Yunnan University, killed his four roommates and ran from police for twenty-one days before he was captured. He was executed three months later.

phone call, I'd rather call my dad, since he at least understands how to set up call waiting. Calling 110 and being told to call back later is enough to make you spit up blood.

With these thoughts in mind, I arrived at my destination. I was busy the moment I got off my bike, so I forgot the matter entirely. When I remembered it later, I blamed myself for not performing a citizen's duty, since my failure to do so might have had serious consequences, even if I wasn't the one who dropped the stones. At the same time, the government didn't do its duty: first, because overloaded trucks have been a problem for years, and second, because these things happen mostly at night. Rocks and mud are also dark in color, and you can't count the number of vehicles and their unsuspecting drivers that have been damaged or involved in accidents due to fallen objects. Is it so difficult to control? Your electronics systems are so advanced that they can tell if a license plate is your mom's or your damn granddad's and whether they're allowed on the road today, and you've got a police force so numerous that they can stop motorbikes during the daily rush hour and load them onto police trucks. You've got so much time on your hands that you can look at the last digit of a license plate to see whether someone's private car is allowed on the road, and you've got the time to inform people with a different last digit that twice each month they're forbidden to drive, but you can't control trucks loaded with mud that leave from a designated place?

All in all, I think that both I and the relevant departments have neglected our duties. I will accept the primary responsibility, but I hope that the relevant departments and the truck responsible will accept their share as well.

LET ME TAKE YOU FOR A U-TURN ON CHANG'AN AVENUE
April 2012

Ten years ago I rented a Xiali* in Beijing. Now, although I was no slouch, I couldn't help it that the car was so slow, so I did what I knew I needed to on the airport expressway: I drove in the slow lane. My friend in the car with me was an angry youth, like me, and right as we were in the middle of a heated debate about corruption and senior officials, an Audi behind us turned on its headlights and sounded a siren. The next lane over was empty, so I continued to drive without moving aside. Not ten seconds later, the Audi turned blood-thirsty: the entire car started flashing, and I got insulted by its loudspeaker. My friend grabbed the steering wheel for a moment and told me, "Let him pass." The Audi shot past us, but its insults persisted for a few hundred meters more. "Man," I said to my friend. "Those bastards may walk crooked, but they drive like a train on a straight line into the darkness." "Forget it," my friend replied. "Did you see how his plate started with 'Beijing AG6X'? That's a pretty powerful number, and it's usually only given to ———. Make sure you watch out for ones starting with A8, too, since those

---

* A compact car based on the Daihatsu Charade and manufactured by FAW Tianjin.

are for ———." All I knew was that you didn't want to mess with drivers with "Shanghai A" plates under 100, so this had me in a fog. Eventually my friend spat out one last comment to that straight-driving Audi train: "Fuck, when I get rich, I have to get a black Audi."

Later, the same friend really did buy a black Audi, but he never got a license plate. "Isn't there a problem with not having a license plate?" I asked. "No," he replied, "because I have this." He pointed to a metal placard in the windshield that read "Police." He later added "Beijing Police," "Great Hall of the People," and "CPPCC." Lined up, the placards stretched over to the passenger side, and during traffic jams we could use them like playing cards. I was most worried about the stack of cards blocking his view. Fortunately, my friend liked to drive fast, so each time he turned a corner, the cards tended to pile up, and we'd have to stop and reshuffle them. I asked him if they worked on the road. "They work fantastically," he said. "Look at me: I don't have a license plate, but I've added these police sirens and flashers, and with all these placards, I'm such a mystery that no cop dares stop me, because no one can guess my background. Here, I'll do an illegal U-turn for you."

We were driving on Chang'an Avenue, a road where it's extremely difficult to do a U-turn. I remember once, not long after I arrived in Beijing, I missed a turn but was unable to turn around. Then I saw a large gate with a broad clearing out in front and, looking closer, I saw that it was Xinhua Gate, the entrance to Zhongnanhai. But to my mind it was part of the Xinhua bookstore chain and thus vaguely connected to my profession. I drove straight in, thinking I could spin a few times in the open space and pretend I had taken a wrong turn. . . . Following a near execution, a deep fear of Chang'an Avenue set in. "Forget it," I said to my friend. "Let's not test it."

My friend didn't answer. When he reached a red light, he turned on his police lights and went directly up to a traffic cop on the road. The traffic cop pretended not to notice and turned his ass to us. "He doesn't care!" I said. My friend raised a corner of his lip and quipped: "He's not getting the hint. Normally, the dumbass would stop the flow of traffic so I can make a turn."

Not one of the cars streaming by let us pass. My friend sounded the siren, and the traffic cop turned to look at us—or, more accurately, at all the plates, which meant he had to stop oncoming traffic. My friend calmly executed a turn. I'll admit, at that moment, twenty-year-old me felt a sense of delight and importance at that privilege, even though it was fake. For about ten seconds I felt unusually inflated, like I was spilling out the window. But I soon realized that no one looked at us with respect and admiration. They were full of indignation. Involuntarily I slunk lower in my seat.

"Don't worry about those idiots," my friend said with disdain. "Did you see that Jetta? Did you see that dumbass's official plate? I knew from the color that it was fake. He bought it at the Siyuanqiao Auto Parts City. But I got mine from my connection with ———. I've heard we're not going to be able to use official license plates in the future. We'll have to have a 'Beijing Police' uniform." He went on: "That dumbass in front of me—why is he driving so slowly? Here, say something into this. Press the button when you speak. Don't say much, just a few words—'Move aside, car in front. Move aside'—and the dumbass will move aside for you."

I can no longer describe the complicated emotions I felt when I sat in the Audi that day. We sat on the roadside at midnight, near Ping'an Avenue, eating lamb hot pot. On the deserted street the cars passed, their strange, drawn-out police sirens wailing. "Dumbass doesn't have the right decibel," said my friend. "They got theirs at the Siyuanqiao Auto Parts City, too."

Yes, we despise privilege when we're faced with it, but when we're enjoying "fake" privileges, we're secretly happy. We judge those susceptible to privilege, but we gloat when we benefit from the same privilege. Lots of people hate special privilege because they don't have it. I have a friend who thinks that if he had privilege, everyone would follow his advice as a matter of course. This isn't necessarily true. I believe everyone gets addicted, unless their privilege is special enough that they need only adopt the subtlest of gestures. My friend has had ups and downs in his life, and he no longer owns that Audi; he drives an extremely ordinary seven-seater family car instead. Talking about the past, he laughed and shook his head and called himself egotistical. "I used to whine about all those people, and now I'm copying them." But he also thought the latest black Audi A8 was gorgeous.

People are always in conflict with themselves. I may be too embarrassed to ever climb into a car with real or fake special privileges and throw my weight around, but every time I'm going to miss a flight, a thought pops up from the darkest part of myself: If I had somewhere I needed to be, and only one flight a day would get me there, and I clearly wasn't going to make it, what if I just happened to have special privileges? Would I make hundreds of passengers wait for me for thirty minutes? Forget hypocrisy, I'd say my answer would be 80 percent yes. And I'd get the captain to blame air traffic control.

No one knows whether they'll ride roughshod over other people and the law, no matter how good or gentle they are. Special privileges afforded to certain individuals cannot be beautified or eliminated through personal cultivation. Even if you are drowning in the spit and hatred of the unprivileged, and no one respects you, you won't be able to stop enjoying what you have. No matter how the common people criticized the Soviet special supply system,† even when public discontent boiled over in the face of economic decline, and destruction seemed imminent, those who were part of the system were unwilling to give it up. No one wants to toss all their vehicle permits to the winds. The answer's not blowing out there.

For a while the USSR fantasized about extending its special supply system to the workers, under the assumption that this would help consolidate power. It never happened that way. And even if that day had arrived, the USSR still wouldn't have ended well. The privileged classes only wanted to extend those privileges to more people out of self-protection because they felt threatened. They had promised others they'd get something that ultimately would be unattainable, because only by limiting the power of those making the promises would the others get their due.

None of this is important, just a reminiscence about my life in Beijing and scribbling a few lines after watching the news. What we see as social progress or regression is often just

---

† Originally intended to ensure that the central government was adequately supplied for basic needs, the system ended up giving party elites access to special stores offering exclusive goods unavailable to the masses. As a spate of food safety scandals were hitting China, Han Han's readers would have been reminded of China's own "special supply system," initiated along the Soviet model, to provide safe food products to the upper leadership.

CHESS PIECES THAT DESERTED THE BOARD
September 2012

A long historical dispute simmering between China and Japan over what are called the Diaoyu Islands by China and the Senkaku Islands by Japan boiled over in 2012. In April, the Tokyo governor's announcement that the municipality would purchase the three main islands from a private family for more than US$25 million, an act China considered illegal, sparked nationwide protests that turned violent in August of that year.

I have a few thoughts that I've reiterated on many previous occasions.

1. I recommend different cars to my friends according to their needs, mostly German ones. Yet many people around me still buy Japanese family-size cars. No one who buys a Japanese car supports a Japanese take-over of Chinese territory; they're thinking about good value, fuel economy, and ease of repair. In the last two years, my friends have bought fewer Japanese cars, but this is only due to currency fluctuations that mean they're no longer cheap. By contrast, prices on many German brands, including even Mercedes-Benz, BMW, and Audi, have dropped into

the 100,000- to 200,000-yuan range. Making money is hard, so value for money always comes first. Japanese cars are always going to be attractive in a society where life's pressures are on the rise.

2. If the authorities had held back for a few days, ordinary people would have come to realize the benefits of "stability," and how *protests* and *gatherings* are dislikable words. "Hey, you want to protest or cause a disturbance? This is what that'll lead to. You want less government control? You hate the police and you hate the army? You're not just going to end up in the gutter—cars are going to be overturned!" And then the machinery of state would start to move and order would be restored, showing that at the critical moment you have to rely on the government. And this would step up the pressure on Japan, too. The government doesn't want war. Use your head: They're set up with all that delicious political power, so who wants a war on their hands? If the foreign enemy isn't a pushover and the war drags on, the national cohesion felt at the start will gradually fade alongside growing domestic unrest, tilting popular sympathies and causing internal fractures, and then you've got big problems. Territory is a big thing for everyone, but resorting immediately to provoking, encouraging, or tacitly approving of impulsive actions by the public doesn't seem like the best idea. As for the Diaoyu Islands, of course they belong to China. Our state hotel is called the Diaoyutai State Guesthouse, and many people in Hong Kong and Taiwan call the islands Diaoyutai, the fishing platform, instead of Diaoyu; so if they were taken by

the Japanese, well, imagine how amusing it would be if the prime minister of Japan received foreign dignitaries in the Great Wall Guesthouse. I actually completely trust the government on this point. As long as Japan doesn't try to push too hard, perhaps stalling is the best policy. Stall for an eternity, and at the rate at which the tectonic plates move, the Diaoyu Islands will eventually conflate with Fujian province, naturally closing the case. In the meantime, perhaps we can sort out some other internal problems.

3. Taking to the streets to express your dissatisfaction with Japan peacefully is perfectly fine. I respect individual choice. There was a time when I would have scoffed at this, but now I neither support nor oppose it. I won't participate, though, since I want to devote my first demonstration to a place that has bullied me and violated my rights more frequently. The ones beating, smashing, and looting must be punished by law, or else I'll have to wonder whether the protests have official backing.

4. My rally race car is a Japanese make. A hot-blooded friend advised me to change to a competing brand and then defeat the Japanese cars to tick them off. I told him that as part of normal rally race, the N4 regulations state that you can pick from only two carmakers, and it's very unfortunate that the other carmaker is also Japanese. The gearbox is from Britain, the shock absorbers are from Sweden, the engine computer is from Australia, the reduction gear is from Germany. The only thing from China is the bag for miscellaneous items next to the car door, but it was all put

together by industrious Chinese workers. That's pretty much how the world runs. In other competitions, I race in a German car, but its brake system, bearings, and many other parts come from Japan. The way to win the world's respect is to manufacture race cars and conversion parts that are of the same quality or even better.

5. If you drive an American or a German car, or run an Italian or a French restaurant, don't think you've done the right thing or opened the right business, or that you've escaped unscathed or removed yourself from the crisis. If China continues to reject reform, there will be many opportunities for international conflicts. It's about territory this time, but who knows what it will be about next time? And don't assume it's safe to use Chinese products, either. Shanghai and Beijing, Guangdong and Jilin—how do you know they won't end up throttling each other? "You overturned my Shanghai VW; I'll smash your FAW VW." Of course, "friendly forces" might get confused and overturn the wrong cars. Disrespect for your countrymen's private property is simply a sign that, in this society, embers turn quickly into flames. No private property is safe.

6. I suggest that when reporting on this serious violation of our countrymen's rights, the news media avoid using the word *patriotism*. This isn't how to love your country. There are respected countries in this world, and other countries that inspire fear, but if we keep going in the same direction, I'm afraid our country will be the only one that inspires laughter. Why not? The concept of "You bully me and my buddy will

bully you" is familiar to me, as is "You bully me and I will bully your buddy," but I've never heard of "You bully me and I'll bully my brother." During my races the last couple of days, even the technicians from Europe knew that there's friction between China and Japan. But I find the pictures of beatings, smashing, and looting completely inexplicable: Is the deed to the islands hidden in a Chinese person's bumper? Is the secret for a nation's rise concealed in the chassis of someone's beloved car? Is the sentiment anti-Japan or anti-China?

7. If hot blood isn't spilled in the right places, it's just chicken blood. Unless you do it right, thousands of people will accuse you of being wrong, even if you're acting on the emperor's orders. If you can't protest about internal issues, protests about external issues won't be convincing. Even if you want to be a patriot, don't be a Patriot missile. When the leaders lose face, we help make them look better; but when the leaders have face, we get slapped. Some people sit on the fishing platform, others are the fish. I love this land, but I don't own an inch of it. I love my country in my own way. Real love brings more respect to the loved one. We shouldn't try to escape punishment in the name of love, brazenly trample on others in the name of love, kill each other in the name of love, or let this country become a joke in the name of love.

8. Don't think that just because you put on a patriot's coat that you're allowed to attack your countrymen and lash out recklessly. Even if no one's stopping you, carrying on won't end well. When the Man's still casting about for a can opener, you're already drunk, and

when the Man's still pouring, you're already on an alcohol-fueled rampage. The Man won't be pleased. The leaders need you slightly tipsy and easily suggestible, rather than at risk of a flare-up. Chess pieces that have deserted the board, even when draped in the national flag, are still deserters.

A VIP'S TRIP TO THAILAND
December 2012

Some time ago, when I received word that I would be going to Thailand to race, I was uncertain: As a racer from the great nation of China, would racing in Thailand be an insult to our national prestige? My friend told me, "Go. Look at it as a beach holiday." I laughed. Can Thailand compare in beauty to China's glorious Hainan Island? After visiting Mohe County in the far northeast and taking a look around the "North Pole Village" last month and seeing the stone marking the Ends of the Earth in Sanya, Hainan, a few years back, you could reasonably say that I've traversed the latitudes. Other countries can only grow longitudinally. Thailand, being south of the Ends of the Earth, must be something special. I made the decision to visit.

Because important travelers from my great homeland have recently been required to observe thrift and economy,[*] I would not fly first class. The flight was scheduled to leave at around 2:00 a.m. I took a car to Shanghai Pudong Airport. No one was on the roads, in the restrooms, or at the security gates, as if they had cleared things just for me. The aircraft was a Sri

---

[*] Han Han is referring to the austerity measures that incoming president Xi Jinping called for Party members and government officials to observe in a speech in early December 2012.

Lankan Airlines Airbus A330-300. I said to Ye Yong, the manager of Shanghai VW 333 who was accompanying me, "Don't go overboard with sponsorship. Stay local and in our own sector." After boarding, we were promoted to first class. This displeased me, since it was our choice as VIPs to fly economy; but if you decide to upgrade us, then not putting us all the way into the cockpit is simply lazy. We may have had to stoop to first class, but I didn't lose face for China: I used an iPad, but the Europeans flying alongside me all used iPad minis.

The airplane landed in Thailand. Clearly a country that's not so friendly toward China, the airport didn't even have a special exit for Chinese tourists. I waited a full three minutes to exit the terminal. The car that arrived to pick us up was a Toyota SUV, so I refused to get in unless the organizers promised me that no crowds would overturn the car because it was Japanese. After I got in, I set a helmet next to me, ready to put it on if any thugs turned up to hit me on the head. But the Thai government made thorough consideration for our safety, and had arranged for Toyotas to fill the streets to confuse the thugs. We arrived at the hotel safely.

I stayed at the InterContinental Bangkok hotel. For certain reasons, important Chinese VIPs aren't allowed to stay in rooms better than a standard en suite, so the presidential suite I'd booked remained empty. Of course, I wasn't going to cancel it myself. It was my choice not to stay there, but I'd have been remiss if someone from another country moved in. After arriving at the hotel, I picked up a banana and started toying with it, and said to the bellboy: "These Thai bananas certainly are smaller than Chinese bananas." "It's a *bashō*," he replied. I said, "The *bashō* comes from China, too. Its earliest record is in *Journey to the West*, when the Bull Demon King's wife uses a fan made out of *bashō* leaves." The bellboy was truly impressed with my knowledge of literary history. Afterward, I gave him a 100-yuan tip, because that was the only change I had.

Using Chinese yuan around the world is ostentatious, so I decided to get some Thai bhat. Thai currency displays a special arrogance: Its largest denomination is 1,000 bhat, ten times larger than ours. Downstairs from the hotel, I called for a taxi and said to the driver: "Take us to seafood." The very diligent driver turned left, then left, then left again, and finally we were at a seafood restaurant. Converted to renminbi, the taxi ride cost about 10 yuan. The restaurant sat beside the railway tracks, or as they say in our country, "A prime location next to the light rail." It was completely empty. My friend asked me if the food might be crap. "They must know our nationality," I said, "and that's why the whole place has been cleared for us." It was stylishly decorated, but there was only one crab to be found. I wondered for a moment whether the crab was for eating, or if it was an offering, and as I dithered, the owner of the restaurant eagerly dragged the crab into a basket. I said, "I presume a crab from your shop will be excellent."

The three of us ordered one crab and three shrimp, and when we got the bill it was 8,200 bhat. Our Thai friends, hearing this over the phone, were shocked: We had been robbed. I said coolly, "We ate four creatures and the undiscounted price was over 10,000. They were showing us respect. It's expensive at any tourist spot if you ask the driver to take you to a restaurant. You've never been to Sanya and haven't seen the state of the market. It's precisely because we're Chinese, a people on the rise, that they're charging us like this. If we were Ethiopian, they wouldn't dare. The crab may have been skinny, but it's the thought that counts, and although the river shrimp were small, we've obtained their respect."

After dinner we decided to go for a stroll and take in

the city. It really is a world of difference from China. The wild dogs everywhere on the streets of Bangkok came off as highly unrefined, but the great aura of the Chinese people was enough that wherever the three of us went, the dogs parted ways. Not a single one bit us. Locals have no concept about a reform economy, for to the Chinese, those were no wild dogs, they were hot pot. The people, dogs, and cats of Thailand passed right by each other on the streets, and squat sheds stood next to Louis Vuitton shops in a highly unharmonious display unbefitting a luxury business.

After walking for about five minutes, we ended up at the hotel. The Chinese physique is excellent, and we walk fast, as everyone knows. After a brief sit-down, it was time to dine again. This time we went to a restaurant right next door. The flavors were great, the crabs huge, and we paid 3,000 bhat for five people. Upon conversion to RMB, it proved the saying: "One hundred to eat your fill, 200 to eat well, 300 to fall over." The surrounding tables had quite a few American and European guests, evidence of the full effect of the global economic crisis, for prices had been lowered in order to cater to them.

Back at my hotel room, I took a seat on the sofa and switched on the television, and found China Central Television. Hearing my native tongue spoken, I was pleased at this manifestation of cultural influence. Contentwise, CCTV was perfectly in line with international standards, and just like European and American stations, it was reporting heavily on the latest American shooting. I lay on my bed, pulled open the curtains, and watched the people and sights down below, the cars passing by, and I found an answer in my heart. No VIP is going to praise a place where you have to pull the curtains by hand. To the sound of the world's concern for American society on the television, I fell indifferently to sleep.

THE PACIFIC WIND
May 2012

The Airbus A320 landed at Taoyuan Airport. The touch-down woke me.

My knowledge of Taiwan doesn't go much beyond the movies of Hou Hsiao-hsien and Edward Yang, although now Wei Te-sheng and Giddens Ko* have added their flourishes. Liang Shiqiu, Lin Yutang, and Hu Shih—writers I like—emigrated to Taiwan, and on top of that, they all fought with Lu Xun. When the mainland was poor, Taiwan was rich, and then when the mainland got rich—or rather, when the government and a small group of people got rich—Taiwan got richer.

War separated one people on two sides of the strait, but the specifics of the tragic separations and happy reunions of individual families have been smoothed over by time. The streets of Taipei, as the band Ukulele sang, "Opened up like a maze in front of me," but every foreign city is a maze for people from

---

* Hou Hsiao-hsien (born 1947) is a prolific filmmaker and a leading member of Taiwan's New Wave Movement, as was Edward Yang (1947–2007). Wei Te-sheng (born 1969) directed *Cape No. 7* (2008) and the historical epic *Seediq Bale* (2011). Giddens Ko (born 1978), a hugely popular online novelist, directed an adaptation of one of his own coming-of-age romances into *You Are the Apple of My Eye* (2010).

somewhere else. Our hotel was right next to the Eslite Bookstore. My friend broke his glasses, so that evening we went to replace them. We took a taxi to an optician's near National Taiwan University. No Taiwanese girls with numbing voices here; the owner himself came out to serve us. My friend liked one pair but was told that he had to wait a few days before they would be ready. "Then forget about it," he said, "I'm only in Taiwan for three days. I need to pick them up tomorrow. I guess I'll go elsewhere." I was shocked by what happened next: The owner took out a pair of contact lenses from a cabinet and pushed them toward my friend, saying, "I'm really sorry I can't help. Use these for your emergency." I usually think the best of people, but my initial reaction was *Shit, this never happens. What's the catch? Will we be able to leave the shop?*

We safely made our way out of the shop and entered the one next door. This owner promised to have new glasses ready the following day, and then put the lenses from my friend's broken glasses in temporary frames, telling him, "You can use these tonight." Both places were ordinary roadside shops that we came across randomly, or else we'd have suspected that our trip organizers arranged the whole thing with the aim of increasing our favorable impression of Taiwan.

There are many small-scale demonstrations and protest banners on the streets of Taiwan, a novel experience for the majority of mainland tourists, many of whom stick by their televisions at night to watch the political debates. When my mother came back from touring Taiwan last year, she told me that she had a great time watching the leaders on television hurl so much invective: It was more fun than the mainland's *Happy Camp* variety show. The Taiwanese, by comparison, found all of this entirely normal. But it was Mr. Wang Songhong, more than Mr. Ma Ying-jeou, the president, who left a deeper impression on me, and he wasn't a celebrity politician or a member of the literati. He was a taxi driver. One morning, my friends and I left the hotel and took his taxi to Yangmingshan National Park. After we got there I realized that I'd left my cell phone in the car. I hadn't recorded the license plate number. My friends helped me contact the taxi company to see if we could get any information, and I called the hotel to ask if they could check their security cameras. After a little while, I received a call from the hotel. "Did you get the plate number?" I asked. They said there was too much CCTV footage and they hadn't found it yet, but a taxi driver had driven back to the hotel just now and turned a cell phone in to reception, saying that one of you had left it in the cab.

I was dumbstruck. I got the name and phone number of the taxi driver and told him I wanted to reward him. "It's okay, that's normal. It's nothing; this is what we usually do," he replied. He told me that a few days earlier he had driven around the island with his friends, and they were planning a trip to the mainland soon. He said he became a taxi driver because he wanted to see the world, and before the conversation ended he said: "I have QQ and Weibo. What's your username? Let's connect on the Net." Immediately I felt a warming of bilateral relations. Then he said, "Do you have Facebook?" "The mainland's lost its Face . . . book," I replied. "Oh, that's right. I have to go. I've got a customer. Let's stay in touch, okay?"

Maybe it's my good luck that everyone I meet is nice, or maybe I've only stepped into shallow waters, so I only meet friendly people. It goes without saying that, had I stayed in Taiwan for a few more days, I would have seen undesirable things: Perhaps they have aging infrastructure, perhaps they have raging populism, perhaps the people never stop complaining, perhaps they have a ton of issues of their own. There

Yes, I have to thank Hong Kong and Taiwan for protecting Chinese culture, preserving the positive traits of the Chinese people, and keeping many essential things free from disaster, even if they can be castigated for various things themselves. And while we may have the Ritz-Carlton, the Peninsula hotel, Gucci, and Louis Vuitton, and while the wives of our county chiefs may be richer than their highest officials—and while they could shoot twenty or thirty films for what it costs to produce one of our major movies; and while Hong Kong and Taiwan will never host the World Expo or the Olympic Games—when I went on their streets and met their taxi drivers, restaurant owners, and passersby, I felt no pride whatsoever. They once had what we have now, their taxpayers wouldn't agree to what we boast about, they've kept what we've discarded, but what brings the most pride is precisely that which we lack.

For a nation, culture, law, and freedom are everything. Other countries won't respect you simply because the wealthy are snapping up supercars and top-notch yachts. Sitting twenty thousand feet in the air in that Airbus A330, an hour and a half away from Shanghai, I looked out the window at the ocean, as far as I could see. We share the Pacific winds, so let them blow over everything.

LIFE AS I KNOW IT

In 2010, Han Han married his long-term girlfriend, Jin Lihua, a film school graduate who had been the producer on his first directorial effort, a music video shot in 2008. Their first child, a daughter named Xiaoye, was born in November of that year. A son followed in 2014. Certain heavy subjects, such as child abuse and China's future, have become more personal to him since becoming a father, as have old topics of indignation such as education. As Han Han ages, he remains a public figure, an important part of the post-'80s set, but no longer an icon of youthful rebellion. He has published successive best sellers, been feted as a public intellectual, and won Driver of the Year three times. Still full of the righteous anger that characterized his teens and twenties, he has become a mentor to a new generation of troublemakers.

LIFE AS I KNOW IT
June 2012

A while ago, a friend I hadn't seen for a long time came to one of my races. He's currently working as the manager for a celebrity. He stayed in my team tent the whole weekend. On Sunday, when it was time to part, he told me I hadn't really developed myself all that well. I had image management issues, and with a professional manager who could take care of them, things would be far better for me than they were now. "So how about I sum all that up in an e-mail when I get home?"

Just now he called and said, "You've got too many problems to clear up in an e-mail. Today's race, for example. Did you know you were in double-reverse the whole time?" This left me baffled. *Double-designation** and *single-reverse* I've heard about, but *double-reverse* was a mystery. Eventually I figured it out: *double-reverse* means your clothes are on backward and inside-out. I said I'd left home in a rush and didn't notice, and there was no one to remind me. No wonder I'd felt a little choked all day.

---

* During investigations of Party members for corruption and other wrongdoing, they can be requested to explain themselves at a designated time and in a designated place. This procedure, similar to house arrest, is colloquially known as "double-designation."

My friend said that wasn't the major problem. "You're just careless, but it invites mockery. What's worse is how you just go to sleep on the couch in your team tent! Altogether, a dozen people came to take pictures of how you slept, five of them with press passes, four from the team, and three of them other drivers. Two of them deliberately took ugly close-ups of your head. I checked them out: Five made Weibo posts. One photo was atrocious, bad enough to hurt your image. You don't have anyone around you to block people from taking pictures: That's absolutely forbidden in our profession." I said I couldn't help it. I'd been up all night watching the Euro Cup and hadn't gotten enough sleep. "Can you teach me how to sleep with airy beauty?" I asked.

My friend continued his lecture. My facial expression was only of secondary importance. "The key thing was that you slept balled up, with a hand stuffed into your crotch. That's image-destroying, obscene behavior, and Internet users would be disgusted if the photo got uploaded and they saw it." I said, "I didn't stuff my hand down the crotch of those Internet users. If I touch my own cock, it doesn't cock-block them, does it? So what if it disgusts them?" My friend said, "You're wrong. You're a public figure, and this era is all about microblogs. Anyone can take a photo, and the crazier it is, the faster it circulates. You need to make sure that no single photo is going to affect your image. Like that one of your hand in the wrong place. It'll get reposted thousands of times, easy." I said there was really nothing I could do. The A/C was on too high, and ever since I was young, whenever it's cold, I sleep in a guard-the-crotch position. I can't just hire a few bodyguards, like I'm a badass, to stop people from taking photos of me whenever I want to sleep.

My friend pointed out a whole bunch of instances, like

taking photos with anyone or signing whatever someone puts in front of me—situations where there could be hidden dangers. I said, "That's not true, I wouldn't sign a 100 RMB note if someone handed it to me." My friend agreed: "Good. You're aware of that much at least. In my industry, some stars will sign money they're handed and then get mocked to death online. It's a bad idea to damage the RMB." I said, "No. I just don't want my name up there next to old Mao."

My friend said sourly, "See, you can't say that sort of thing whenever you like. You'll offend too many people. You're the same way when talking with your team. You'll say anything, and you're always cursing. You've got to understand that if anyone has ulterior motives and records a little of that on a mobile phone, it'll be huge negative news if it goes online. Do you know how many people were in the tent? Eighteen. Do you know them all?" "I don't know a few of them," I said. My friend nearly dropped his handset. "You talk like that in front of people you don't know? Have you even considered the consequences? You took a photo with someone right after you woke up, with all that Teletubby hair, and there was even a flash. You can imagine how that turned out. Your clothes don't match. You look like a peasant. Worse than that, you're sloppy: You need to zip your fly. You're too slack, and without a professional manager to keep a tight, systematic rein on your image, you won't be able to preserve any sense of mystery or celebrity cachet. If you're positioned well, if you have suitable people to handle operations for you, and if you adjust your social circles, you'll be able to earn far, far more. Tell me, how do you plan on marketing yourself? What do you think?"

I said, "I've had one question in mind the whole weekend. I'm 0.3 seconds behind my opponent, so how am I going to catch him? I'm lucky if I remember to put on clothes before going out, let alone have them match."

I hung up, and then in the still of the night I thought over what my friend had said. He was right about some things. The entrance to my tent isn't barred. It's open to everyone, so there really *would* be a problem if someone wanted to stealthily take a video or a recording, or liveblog the situation. Your "original factory settings" decide whether you're going to guard against strangers. I like to start off by assuming that everyone is good and then screen out the bad people, but some people are the opposite. My "screening method," though, is letting them sucker me once. I believe in honest dealing, but I also trust in bad luck and taking it on the chin.

About my clothes: I bought ten white T-shirts this summer, and two black leather jackets the previous winter. Shoes: I'm looking at one or two pairs, since I'm headed to a race, not a beauty contest. It matters to me if the car gets smashed up, but I really don't care if I'm wearing ugly clothes.

Life as I know it means whatever I make of it, except for the rumors. To me good fortune is how much culture you can create. Beating odds of a 100 million to 1 thirty years ago and winning out over all the other sperm, I'm awesome by virtue of being born, so I need to make a mark on the world. I recognize that being well dressed and looking elegant creates a good impression, but that's not my area of expertise. I recognize that, in this society, many people think that so long as you don't swear, then lies, empty promises, clichés, and flagrant and crazy rumors are morally acceptable, but I feel the opposite. To those sanctimonious morons I have but one thing to say: Fuck. Yeah, that'll make the moral fear-mongers tremble and shout criticism and roll around on the floor, then leap up and start judging. That's solved by saying it again: Fuck! Yeah, it's a fuck-you, but not a fuck-you to you or your family. It's a fuck-you to the world, a world that has no problem with false but genteel accusations; a world in which the unethical can be moral judges if they avoid foul language; a world where people whose speech is clean but whose hearts and hands are not hold sway; a world that arbitrarily confuses black and white and right and wrong; a world where a public figure—or anyone at all, really—shouldn't say *fuck*. Well, fuck that world all over.

Life as I know it means doing the things you like and taking care of yourself and your family. Life isn't scaling a mountain or descending to the depths of the sea. It's the way you look when you sleep on a regular bed. I don't think there's any imperfect beauty in having regrets, as the saying goes; but, by contrast, there's beauty in screwing up. My hobbies aren't limited to writing and racing. I do lots of other things, some of which I'm not very good at, and I fail. I'll tell my friends, "I really like it, and I've done it before, but it doesn't suit me. It's embarrassing." What I hate is hearing someone say, "If I'd done it, I'd definitely have been better than so-and-so." Nuts to that. Every time I'm a success on the podium, I've screwed up ten times off it, but so what? I haven't died, and I keep at it. People only remember your successes.

Life as I know it means being with people you like. Once I saw a girl at a fast-food joint, but hesitated for five minutes because I didn't have the guts to talk to her. She ended up leaving, and I regret it to this day. Right then I was an idiot. What would it have mattered if I went over? Worst-case scenario: Her boyfriend comes out of the bathroom. Rather than dying someday regretting not doing this or that, why not be able to boast of my success at something and mock myself for failing something else? I've got plenty to do now, being with my family, my wife and kid, and racing almost twenty times a year. I'm also starting a new novel and a travelogue, and aside from the occasional trip to the studio for a magazine shoot, I don't have much time or effort to spend on dressing up, much less the mental space to think about improving my mediocre image and positioning. I'm only taking baby steps. I'm in charge of producing things, not user experience or post-sales, and other people's tastes can't dictate my work. If you like my writing, it's a bright day. If you don't like my writing, it's still a bright day. I thank my friend for his meticulous advice, and I know that I may lose out due to my personality and lifestyle choices and will face unknown consequences. But at least I've never given up anything, from the tiniest flashes of inspiration to my grand ideals, and although my life may be filled with frustration or remorse, I have few regrets. My friend, I thank you for all that you said. There are millions of loves and countless hearts out there in the world. It's my good fortune if some of them come my way, but it's also no misfortune if they don't. I do recognize one thing, though: No matter how much of a hurry you're in, when you go out, you've got to zip up your fly.

FATHERHOOD

From Beijing Youth Weekly
July 2012

On His Daughter

BYW: On living, when you mentioned earlier that you don't try to please anyone, there are probably exceptions, right? Your daughter, for example. The label "father" is one we haven't brought up yet.

Han Han: "Father" is a seal, not a label.

BYW: Has life changed much for you since having a daughter?

Han Han: Not all that much, fortunately.

BYW: You've written what looks like a love letter to your daughter: "My only wish is for my daughter to be happy. It doesn't matter whether she succeeds in the Chinese sense. So long as she has good character, I am willing to do everything to make it possible for her. I am willing to create a world for her so she doesn't need to suffer in a cruel and wicked society. Naturally, she should do whatever she wishes, and try anything she likes, and I'll just be the safety net when she takes risky climbs. If, due to some future misfortune, I have trouble taking care of her, then

I won't object to being a chauffeur for Robin Li, grinding ink for Bai Ye, or holding lights for Chen Kaige.* I'd like to have more children, of course, and if I have a son, then he'd have to suffer, to yoke himself to reality and work hard for himself and in order to change society, to fight to build a safe environment for the daughters of the world." These are warm feelings, but some people will no doubt suspect that you have serious male chauvinist tendencies, and that you think of girls as weak.

Han Han: Isn't that the case? People have all sorts of roles the world over, but some things are simply the way they are. In many areas, like walking on a dark road in the middle of the night, or in athletic competitions, girls suffer. I'm a protector of girls. I don't want my wife to go out to work, and I want to protect my daughter. If you want to call that male chauvinism, then I'll admit to it.

BYW: If your daughter doesn't want to go to college when she grows up, or if there are other issues, will you interfere?

Han Han: There will definitely be lots of issues to face. She'll have her rebellious period, and quite likely will knit a sweater for some idiot. I could keep her forever, but no one wants to be kept forever, even by their own father. We all want society's approval, after all. Three things are critical: Don't be a burden to society, don't be a burden to your parents, and gain the skills to survive on your own. Skills are particularly important. That way it

---

* On occasion, Han Han has been critical of Robin Li, the CEO of Internet search engine Baidu; Bai Ye, a prominent literary critic; and Chen Kaige, a major film director.

doesn't matter whether you go to school. It's easy to imitate dropping out of school: You could fill out a withdrawal application, or simply stop going for a month and drop out automatically. Not going to school doesn't take guts. Imitating guts is what takes guts. So I hope that my daughter will gain the skills to survive in society. I won't interfere with her schooling, but I will interfere with her skills and abilities.

BYW: Do you usually do housework? Do you think you're a good husband and a good father?

Han Han: I don't do housework. I'm pretty careless in my life, and as long as I don't break anything or cause any other problems, that's a net positive. (*Laughs.*) But I'm definitely a good husband and father. I do have guilt, of course. I'm used to writing in the middle of the night, and then I need to have a snack at 3:00 a.m., so my wife always gets up to make it for me. It's a habit that she's gradually gotten used to over the years. She also takes care of lots of other things. So I feel guilty for that, and also for not spending enough time with my daughter at the age when she's the cutest.

BYW: As I understand it, you have nearly twenty races a year, and this takes up quite a bit of your time. And you also have to deal with online debates, like the one that boiled over at the start of the year.

Han Han: Two races a month, or twenty-some a year, and each one takes about a week. So I don't have enough energy for my kid, and I've missed her cutest period. Besides, at the beginning of the year I was stupid enough to pay attention to that lunatic and trap setter. Like an idiot, he had me writing essays to prove my own innocence, because when someone accuses you of doing something you haven't done, it already shows that he has bad motivations. I always think the best of people. I imagine them to be kind and innocent, but wicked people really do exist. So I wasted time on that stuff and played with those ugly people instead of my own cute kid! Public power may have a bottom line, but the ugliness of people doesn't!

I CAN'T AND I DON'T
June 2007

Reading lots of comments this year, I've discovered that many of our compatriots are pretty weird.

I said, discussing the issue of young love, "Once you know what love is, then making love is a natural right that no one can interfere with." Decent folk replied, "No, I don't have that right." And then they retorted, "What would you do if your six-year-old son had sex with my three-year-old daughter?" The question baffled me, since I'd never thought about such a seedy what-if.

I said, "Writing is a talent you're born with. Anyone can write once they've learned to speak, but not through the training of writing essays at school." And decent folk replied, "No, I don't have that talent." And then they retorted, "If you didn't learn to write essays at school, how are you able to form phrases into sentences?"

I said, "Math doesn't give you the ability to think logically. That came with your brain when you were born." Decent folk replied, "Cut the crap. It didn't come naturally for me. I had to learn how to find the shaded area before mastering logical thinking."

You all don't really have a high opinion of yourselves, do you?

Anyhow, people will always deny it when someone tells

them, "You have this right; you have that ability." They'll say, "Don't you poison the thoughts of others."

But there are also exceptions. For example, if someone says that everyone's actually allowed to say "No," they're all going to accept that, although they'll limit themselves to saying "No" to the person who told them that.

CHILDREN'S DAY
June 2012

I was in the south, preparing for all sorts of races, when one day I realized we were coming upon Children's Day. A dozen years ago, I once looked forward to getting presents on Children's Day myself, but today I'm worried about what to give my own daughter. I'm befuddled. There are a few racers from my generation in ordinary financial situations who make extra dough by going to events around the country when they're not racing. They do this so they can give the best things to their children. There are quite a few playboys in my racing circles, too. In the past, after we were done racing in Zhuhai, we'd go gambling in Macau. Now that we have kids, we've switched to buying milk powder in Hong Kong, all because China whispers to us: "Nothing here is reliable, so earn more money, and then, if you can, emigrate."

I've written a lot over the last few years, and I've read a lot of news. My deepest concern is this: China should feel the most sorry toward children. I'm talking about everything from birth planning to the melamine scandal, from child prostitution to the Karamay fire, from food safety to test-focused education, from the Xiao Yueyue case to schoolbuses.* A country

---

* Several dairy companies were involved in a 2008 scandal in which infant formula adulterated with melamine in order to increase its

that claims to be in an age of prosperity has not sufficiently protected its children, whether in the cities or the rural areas. . . . Just as when natural disaster strikes, the most unfortunate victims are always children studying in their school dormitories. In the past I'd be outraged, but now that I have a daughter and I read the news every day, I get so caught up in it that I can't help myself and rage around the room. Apart from wishing all the children of the world Happy Children's Day, I also have a few words to say as a new father. There is some buzz I need to kill:

1. We must remove the charge of child prostitution. This charge was added ten or so years ago, and it can apply very broadly. It appears with high frequency, and it's often used to get out of other charges. A girl is a girl, rape is rape, so what does *child prostitution* mean? Shove some money at her after the rape, and suddenly you're a client, not a rapist, and the child is transformed from victim to prostitute? Whatever the cause, even if the child was hoodwinked by some organization, the way to handle it that befits human nature is charging it as rape and heavily punishing the perpetrators. This is an evil law and it must be revoked. Only two days ago, another young girl was sexually assaulted in Zhejiang province, but it was ruled to be child prostitution. Yet today we're celebrating

---

apparent protein content led to kidney stones and renal failure. Xiao Yueyue, or Wang Yue, was a two-year-old girl run over by two vehicles on October 13, 2011, in Foshan, Guangdong, and subsequently ignored by passersby.

Children's Day. If I search key words about this on Weibo right now, the search terms will be blocked. Is this the way that our country protects its young girls? I will fight this evil law to the end.[†]

2. In place of this evil law, add a kinder law forcing the use of infant seats in cars. As a car racer, I'm fully aware of the impact of a crash. Many people sit in a car holding their baby, imagining that in the event of an accident, their arm strength is unsurpassable. There are folks all around me who won't think seriously about putting their kid in a safety seat, but I caution them to do so at every possible opportunity. And in return, they only say, "Oh, well, it'll be okay. We drive slowly." This is a huge misunderstanding. Without the protection of the safety seat, even at 30 kilometers per hour, the kid could get hurt or even be thrown from the car. Tragedies come thick and fast, so a new law should be created. A warning or even punishment should be handed out if a child under the age of three is riding in a car without being in a safety seat.

There are so many other things we can do for kids. These are just the top priorities. As for Children's Day presents, the poor have one way of celebrating, and the rich have another. Presents grow old, Children's Day will pass, but poisonous milk powder, poisonous food, poisonous air, abducted children, children who can't afford to go to the hospital, students

---

[†] Revisions to the Criminal Law of the People's Republic of China that were passed in August 2015 and took effect on November 1 that year abolish the crime of patronizing child prostitutes.

who are treated like political props—they surround us, alive and breathing. On this day, if a high official goes to visit some school, I bet there will be kids beating waist drums and waving red flowers, lined up in two rows, rain or shine.

So in this land where children are not sufficiently protected and where harm to children does not merit punishment, June 1 is celebrated as Children's Day. Many other days are Crimes Against Children Day. Apart from suggesting that we abolish the charge of child prostitution and force people to use child safety seats, I also suggest we make the first of the next month Children's Day, too, and the first of the month after that. I've always thought that the reason we work so hard is so we're around for the arrival of the days of glory. As long as the next generation gets to live in a better world, I'm happy. When my daughter has her own kid, if the world is still as it is now, I can only say that there won't be much to celebrate for National Day on the first of October, we so might as well change it to Children's Day, too.

THE NEW MASTERS HAVE ARRIVED
July 2012

The building of a copper smelting plant in Shifang, Sichuan province, prompted large-scale demonstrations during which citizens stormed government buildings, and police employed stun grenades and tear gas to disperse them. Many commenters at the time were impressed that, unlike previous protests, young people from around Sichuan, especially the post-'90s generation, were eager to play a pivotal role in the demonstrations.

Today, Shifang is all over the news, but I can't tell what's real from what's fake. What I *can* be certain of is that Shifang is in trouble, and aid has arrived from everywhere. Folks born in the 1990s are impressive. Last night, they stood outside the Shifang government demanding the students' release. Students from Guanghan came forward because many of those arrested came from there. Other people said that the situation was sparked by students demonstrating outside the government gates. So it's a good thing that all but six students have been released. It's said that people have changed their minds about the post-'80s generation. Now the Shifang incident is changing their minds about the post-'90s.

The post-'90s generation aren't just "anti-mainstream" because they sport explosive haircuts. Police "bombs" are much more violent than those perms. They also used flash grenades; if you're a boy, you're familiar with these from *Counter-Strike*. Our horizons have been broadened. The despotic nature of the local government has been exposed: They use stun grenades on their own people. Strong flashes may cause momentary dizziness, but terrible actions can't be covered up. Do you think you're making *Men in Black 4*? They should know that each flash of light freeze-frames that historical moment, and there's no way to eradicate it.

I have no objection if a citizen who has done wrong is detained and punished by law. But don't you think police should apologize if they go overboard and use their weapons on citizens? On the government's "Shifang Alive" official Weibo account, their tone has never wavered, remaining as hard and unapologetic as if they are handing down imperial law from on high. They even came out with slogans such as "Strongly defend the legal rights of the masses, strongly defend the overall harmonious stability of society," which is totally impossible, like trying to sing while playing the harmonica. I want to say there's progress even though the account is obviously still slinging insults. For example, the official account uses a sexually frigid tone to address a bunch of hormonal young adults, and they are not lying too much. In contemporary China, this is rare. The blogger even knows how to use the "long *weibo*"—a tool for attaching a long essay to microblog—which is as new and strange as an official suddenly saying: "Damn the regulations!" Encouragement should be made each time there's progress. Then . . . the criticisms can continue.

Back to the post-'90s students. They ought to be praised. But let's also reflect. In a set of photos, I saw a slightly injured post-2010s toddler, and so, as the father of a one-year-old, I got very angry at the army and the police. I stayed up all night and wrote the essay, "The Release of Shifang." Always protect yourself and your family. Your kids shouldn't be out there: This isn't a temple fair, a party, or a riot. Everything we do, we do for our children. I can eat "gutter oil,"* but I don't want my daughter to; I can breathe terrible air, but I don't want my daughter to. I can live in ———, but I don't want my daughter to. I used to think that the post-'80s and post-'90s were wasted generations, but now I think perhaps we can finish what our predecessors started. They are the new masters. These people are the new masters of the future. They're here. The world is yours, and ours, but in the end it's theirs.

Some people say that I could write about the Shifang incident only because there were so many political games involved. It's true, but I don't care. If there's wine tonight, why not get drunk? If the bottle has been opened, then why not drink it? Play all you want: I want rights. Most people feel like they're in the same boat, and protest because of the environment we live in. On the path to a better and more democratic country, we stand up, walk outside, sit down; we're not doing this merely for vague and empty words, but perhaps for one thing, one person, one tree, one factory. Perhaps we're invested in the incident, or perhaps we aren't. Just as Shifang's pollution will never float to Shanghai, I'm certain that every person in front of their computer will experience a day like this. And when that day comes, we'll also need your understanding and support, my friends from afar.

---

* This term refers to waste oil that is reprocessed and resold as cheap cooking oil.

CHUNPING, I DID IT
December 2012

When I left Longyou in Zhejiang province, the weather was raining like it had in years past. If not for the rally race, I don't think I would ever have set foot in that county town. I always drove there at two in the morning, and I'd always head to Yang Aizhen's food stall to have a bowl of little wontons. I always left on a Monday at noon, and I'd buy some food to take with me to eat in the car. I have to admit that the KFC in Zhejiang tastes a little spicier than the one in Shanghai.

Ten years ago, I formally launched my rally racing career. The first race was in Sheshan Hill, Shanghai, and what had been the rally leg back then is now a five-star hotel and villas at the foot of the hill. The leg started at what is now Le Royal Méridien Shanghai hotel, went straight for a few hundred meters, and then turned toward what today is the Moon Lake Park, the gathering spot for reporters and spectators. I remember, the night before the 2003 race, I had an infinite number of fantasies about how the first turning point in my life would appear: Would it come as an entirely standard straight race line, a dazzling drift, or would I simply execute a textbook turn? What happened was that I didn't brake. The first turn of my career began by backing up.

Soon the tournament reached Longyou, a gravel stage. When I was younger I used to dream about rally racing. My teenage eyes were transfixed by the sight of rally drivers doing high-speed drift turns in the mountain forests. From then on, I resolved to be like them. People never want to admit that they had idols as adolescents, but they forget the power idols hold during childhood. When I buckle my seat belt and put on my helmet, I feel like I'm possessed by that earlier generation of rally drivers I so idolized.

Then, on my first rally leg, I drove into a ditch.

Lots of people laughed at me, of course. In my first year of racing, my finances had a hard time of it. The 2004 racing season was particularly difficult: I withdrew from a friend's private team and no one wanted me, and I had to repair my car on my own. I'd nearly spent through my accumulated book earnings, and since I was so engrossed in racing, I had no inclination to write. With nothing in reserve, the only thing I could do was restrict spending on food, clothing, and lodging. Coincidentally, at that time my car buddies in Beijing were well-off, so sometimes I didn't even dare go out to dinner with them. One friend who came from a family in real estate saw I had no fixed address, so out of goodwill he said that he could sell me an apartment along the Second Ring Road, over a hundred square meters for over a 100,000 yuan. I had under a hundred thousand left in my bank account that I was planning to spend on the next few racing stages, so I turned him down without a second thought. I had the notion that whatever I strove for, it should at least be in service of my childhood dreams. Being a landlord never seemed part of my dreams. And so I resolved to buy myself some tires, and in the course of buying them I ran across a kind person who brought me my very first sponsorship deal: Michelin decided to give me six tires.

Nothing more than six tires, but I was excited as hell, since Michelin was a major international manufacturer. Ah, my first step toward bad-assitude. Those six tires were worth around 10,000 yuan, and I contributed a few thousand of my own to do up a huge sticker that covered my entire car with their logo. My navigator didn't understand, so I told him it was an "emotional investment." Although it wasn't a large sponsorship, putting up the sticker would make them feel I was loyal. "That's a canny Shanghainese for you," my friends said. "Whatever. I'm just taking the long view," I said.

When the race started, the guy who gave me the tires ran over looking a little uncomfortable. "Bro," he said, "we're just giving you a helping hand. We don't need this kind of pay-back."

"It's not a big deal. Help me with a drop of water, and you'll get a whole spring in return," I replied.

He seemed about to say something but then left.

After that, I received a message asking me if I could take off the sticker, because foreigners from the tire company headquarters had arrived and were quite displeased when they noticed an unknown car plastered with their logo. Michelin had very strict sponsorship rules, and they typically only sponsored winning drivers. "We don't ask for compensation for helping you, but putting our brand on your car is easily misunderstood."

I stood there for a few seconds. "I don't have the time now. Wait until the first day is over and I'll take it off." But it turned out that in the first stage the shocks on my old clunker went out after a few kilometers. I was a driver with practically no mechanical knowledge, so I just dropped anchor and popped the hood and pretended to take a look inside as a show of professionalism. It was the latest in a series of races I'd dropped out of because my car had broken down, and at that point I was being passed by other drivers in brand-new cars. I longed to be buried by the dust they kicked up. At that moment my mobile phone rang. It was my friend calling. "I heard you dropped out again," he said. "Don't be depressed. Oh, and have you taken off the sticker?"

That was the first time I cried over a rally race. You know, when you're a competitive person, if you ever do poorly at something, mockery might affect you. Too ashamed to return to the race pit, I stealthily towed the car back to a repair shop.

Unlike those inspirational films, I didn't make a comeback in the next race. In the first stage, my car blew a cylinder when the piston punched a big hole in the cylinder body, and the engine compartment caught fire. Even though I couldn't afford another engine, under the light of the flames, I no longer felt sad. What's solid needs to be tested in fire, and those flames would neither warm my body nor burn up my heart. From that day forth, I had something to do. Everyone's body has its tough spots, which are different for each person. Some people's tough spots are hand calluses, others' are spots on the back, and others' are lines on their faces. My own toughness is the muscle of my heart. I'll die before I give up, and expire before I relax. You want to turn the people who laugh at you into the butt of the joke.

After the engine burned out, I went back home. My neighbor and childhood friend Han Chunping (as for why Chunping's parents gave him a girl's name, your guess is as good as mine) said to me, "You may be a fair bicyclist, but driving to win a national competition is tough, even if we all recognize you're the fastest in Tingdong village." I said, "Let's wait and see."

Here's what happened: 2012 marks my tenth year in rally competition. In Longyou, where I'd dropped out of competition that first time, I hoisted my third Driver of the Year trophy. More gratifyingly, I could finally tell Chunping that I'd done it. Once is a fluke, twice might be luck, but the third time showed I was pretty good. Unfortunately, since I started too late, my skills are limited, and while I might not be too shabby among Asian rally drivers, I can't compare to the Europeans. Our environment is inadequate, and so am I. Perhaps seated at the computer reading this essay right now is someone with the innate talent to stand astride the world, and he might not even have a driver's license.

I've come to understand many things. People may laugh at you, but that's normal, both subjectively and objectively speaking. When you don't do well, or if you haven't finished something, then what exempts you from mockery? Your tears and your misfortune? Your unique set of difficulties? Everybody appeals to God, everybody sometimes feels like they're not going to make it. When others encourage you, that's your fuel. When they mock you, it could be a fuel additive. I didn't end up becoming enemies with the reporters who mocked me. We're good friends now. And although my car's plastered with stickers from different sponsors these days, and although I have an unlimited supply of the best tires from Pirelli or Yokohama, drive the best racing car, and use the best parts every race, I still remember those six tires. Back then I felt like I had to live up to expectations and prove my strength, but now I feel like I ought to simply be grateful to them—not because they gave me a morale boost, but because they've done good. They've helped drivers with potential while maintaining their own commercial principles, and if I were the policy maker, I'd do the same thing. When you know you're able, and others might think you have a chance, cut the crap and do it already. Complaining is meaningless. When you don't let your own light shine, you can't blame other people for lack of vision.

When I fail, I don't get depressed. My childhood fantasy did not involve winning a title, at least, but just being in a rally car and driving like my idols did. I knew that the road was long and that victory might not bring me any glory, since others might think the National Rally Championship a fake competition if a writer wins the grand prize. It's a valid opinion formed out of ignorance but not out of malice. Still, who cares? There will always be people for whom F1 is the only kind of racing, and Pelé is the only soccer player. To hear them tell it, Bill Gates is the only one in the world who knows business. If you do A, they'll ask why you didn't do B, and when you've done B, they'll ask why you haven't done C. You don't need to prove yourself to these types, or even say anything at all. You need only to ignore them and keep going. Action is your principle, and running off their mouth is their right. History will record your work and your achievements but won't leave behind anything of their gossip.

This essay is dedicated to my 2003–2012 rally seasons, to every friend who worked hard and never said quit, to every car I crashed into, to my family and friends who have always prayed for me to drop out, to the teammates and technicians who fought beside me, and to Xu Lang, the king of rallies, who died in 2008. From you I learned how to drive, and your shadow falls over every move I make in a race. You let me know that some things won't be obliterated, you taught me to laugh at it all, you let me understand that no matter how many people in the world try to discredit you, no matter how dark the world becomes, all you have to do is smile. Grin big, because your teeth are always bright.

REMEMBERING XU LANG
June 2008

Xu Lang is gone.

He was China's best rally driver, a two-time winner of the rally car of the year competition. I met Xu Lang in 2002, when I'd just started rally racing and couldn't drive, and when the best thing to do was to sit in a master's car. His team back then was Shanghai VW 333, like me. I drove my broken-down vehicle to Zhejiang province, to Wuyi, his birthplace. Riding in his car, I finally understood how you should drive in a rally race. I was able to make good stage times from then on.

After that, I went to Xu Lang's house once or twice a year. He was the most mischievous yet strongest and most prudent Chinese driver I've ever come across, and he was my best friend. He'd serve tea every time I went over. I've never liked the stuff—I drink water, and I can't tell good tea from bad—which meant I had to amuse myself with teasing his dog. The dog kept chasing after Xu Lang's mother's chicken and spent lots of time in a cage, so it treasured every minute of freedom. Later on, when Wenzhou held a short-track race, he brought a new Labrador to the track. We both won our groups in the race, the last formal race of the previous year, and both of us were quite pleased.

Last year he and a few friends formed a team called Nameless, and on several occasions invited me to join. But I said, "You're using your own money, which puts pressure on me. It won't be easy for you to criticize me if I crash, and it'll be even harder for me. Once you've gotten sponsorship, I'll definitely join up." After all, it was pretty interesting racing and messing around with him. He was an extremely loyal person, and he loved to joke. His favorite joke was asking someone in front of their girlfriend, "Didn't you bring a different girlfriend last time?" and then adding, "What are you kicking me for?"

Xu Lang may have possessed the greatest innate talent and the best skills out of all the Chinese drivers I know, but he was also the hardest working, and the most willing learner. There are lots of categories to racing, and whenever he saw a good track racer or an off-road driver, he'd ask them for advice. He'd been to the Shanghai Tianma Circuit twice, once with his own car and once in a rented one, and he compared notes with me about asphalt driving, modestly telling me the whole time that he wanted to learn from me. Just a month ago at the Shanghai Rally, he was China's fastest Group N asphalt racer, but when his clutch slipped the next day and he went overtime in repairs, he was penalized three minutes and dropped from a sizable lead to fourth place. "Damn it," he said. "If I'd known, I'd have given it a gentle start today, since I was leading by so much anyway."

The last time I took Xu Lang to dinner was before that race. We were in a hurry to finish before heading to the drivers' meeting but had no place to park, so we parked illegally in front of a closed shopping center, and went somewhere else to eat. We bet on whether we'd be ticketed before we finished eating. Xu Lang said, "Ticketed," and I said, "I guess I'll have to say not ticketed. Let's make it a hundred, and I'll pay up if I lose." I ended up winning that hundred, and I've been trying to think of a way to lose it again. Regrettably I'll never get the chance.

Before he left Shanghai, we went to the Tianma Circuit to see motorcycles, and I said, "I want to buy one." He said, "You buy that one, and I'll buy an identical one, and someday we'll ride to Tibet."

"I just drove out there. Riding would be pretty tough, wouldn't it? And look at this bike. It's not comfortable. Our girls will feel uncomfortable riding it," I said.

"We'll have a repair car follow behind, and they can ride in that," he said.

"Okay," I said. "But I've got to buy an enormous ATV half the size of a car. Got one at home?"

"They've expanded the factory you saw last time you came out. They've got everything now. When I get back from Russia, we can check out their motorcycles. They've also got remote-control boats. . . ." he replied.

I'm a pretty free person, I think, but I sometimes envied his lifestyle and attitude. He was one of China's elite racers, the best equipped to fight it out with the supporters of European rally champions, but he never made making money his primary goal. He said, "Everything I earn is a loss in the end, since I've got to spend tons on training every year, and I have to spend my own money to enter international races. It'd be better to seek happiness in domestic races. But I'm afraid of growing unhappy on the team, so why not get a rally team going with me in the future, with sponsorship we find ourselves? Ignore the boss's moods and race however you want and change whatever parts you like."

At the Shanghai race, he said that even though the Nameless team didn't have sponsorship, they still planned to donate 500,000 yuan to a drive organized by the Federation of Automobile Sports of the People's Republic of China, or FASC, but once they saw that other teams donated less, they decided to lower that amount to avoid any awkwardness. Besides, if they could donate that much as a team with no sponsors, would that make it harder for them to find some in the future? Would they always be a nameless team?

I had to laugh, and said, "So when's that sponsorship coming?"

Last year's Dakar Rally was canceled, so everybody switched to the Trans-orientale Rally. I had to wonder: Would things still have happened like this if Dakar hadn't been canceled? Xu Lang's performance in the 2006 event, nineteenth place, was the best any Chinese driver did in the Dakar, as it's called, although he wasn't satisfied with it himself. He would only have been satisfied with a top-ten finish. "Their cars are totally different," I said. "They're long cars straight from the factory: all steel tube, able to drive off after a three-story fall. Yours—you've only tweaked it a little."

He'd gone abroad quite a few times to train and try out for that Dakar, and when he returned he said, "That was a great car this time. Thrilling. My first time in it, I nearly flipped it on the first turn. . . . You really ought to try an off-road race."

"I'd do it in a factory car, but I like rallying better. It's more exciting, and it's faster."

"This is fast, too. You've got to give it a try," he replied.

The past few days I've taken a daily look at news about the Trans-orientale Rally. Xu Lang was fast, as usual. He was in the top ten, and in an earlier stage he came in fifth with the best stage time of any Chinese driver in international off-road racing. I wanted to call up and congratulate him, but over in Russia his phone was unreachable. Yesterday, as he was helping someone tow a car, the tow cable snapped and the tow hook struck him in the head. Ten minutes later he was carried off by helicopter.

When I heard he was seriously injured I made a bunch of calls but didn't get any details. Friends asked me, too, and I said in consolation, "It's nothing. He's got helmet protection. Maybe it hit him in the face and knocked him out, or at worst knocked out a few teeth and ruined his looks. He'll just have a harder time chasing girls now." It was a shame that he wouldn't be competing, but I still felt that it wasn't a big deal. I wanted to ask him when he got back what it was like to ride in a helicopter, since I felt that a fun-loving guy like him might fall in love with them, and he'd come back looking to make money by anticipating the opening-up of China's low-altitude airspace.

Even this morning, when I was talking on the phone to a friend from the FASC who said Xu was still unconscious, I thought, *That's some effective anesthesia.* But when I learned that he'd taken off his helmet when he got out of the car, I got very worried.

Just now I learned that, due to the seriousness of his injuries, rescue was ineffective. He passed away.

Xu Lang was always an optimist, one of the most optimistic and hospitable people I've ever met. He was never pessimistic, no matter what sort of accidents and breakdowns befell him in his worst seasons; and if he withdrew from a race, he'd wait at the switchback of the slowest ascent and come running over when he saw my car, just so he could give me a high-five. After the race, we'd brag to people that during the course of the race we'd managed to complete a conversation and a handshake.

When he became more consistent, he rarely withdrew, but in the event that he did so, it was always from the top position, since he was so fast. His optimism infected me, and later on, when I had to withdraw while in the lead, I never tried to spread the blame. It was just the price you had to pay on the road to victory. We came to race for our own pleasure, which meant racing lost all meaning if we weren't happy.

Last year, when Colin McRae* died suddenly, Xu Lang was very upset. Now he, too, is gone. I wonder if, in some other world, there's a showdown going on right now between him, McRae, and Richard Burns. The cars over there would be as fast as the ones here, but they'd never break down. He's a hero of Chinese racing, the best professional driver in China, and he died on the raceway in the pursuit of what he loved. Apart from dying of old age, it's the best way for a hero to go, and I hope one day to go that way myself. Coming so early, it's a tremendous loss for Chinese racing, but he is already its greatest legend. I feel honored to have been his friend and to have learned so much from him. There's a lot of what I learned from him in my gravel driving. My one wish is that I can go on to complete what he left unfinished, including the off-road racing he told me about. I've never really enjoyed it in the past, but I think I'll give it a go someday. And I hope that I can dedicate plenty of victories to Xu Lang, to that legendary figure of Chinese racing, to my best friend. I offer up my sincere, highest respect. Rest in peace.

---

* Colin McRae (1968–2007) was a Scottish rally driver who won the World Rally Championship in 1995, 1996, and 1997. Richard Burns (1971–2005) was an English rally driver who won the World Rally Championship in 2001.

SCHOOL REUNIONS
November 2007

I attended my junior high school reunion last Saturday. I'm uneducated and missed a lot of school, so I have half as many classmates as everybody else. Reunions for senior high classmates are more stressful, because I repeated the first year of senior high and spent one year with each group. Every time I enter a roomful of senior high classmates, I have to pull someone aside and ask everybody's names, since not being able to call them by name would have terrible consequences. Junior high reunions are a little better, since I was there for the full three years.

This year's reunion was held in my old classroom, with our homeroom teachers Cai and Peng. I've raced cars for four years and have drifted about for seven or eight, so I imagined I had great psychological strength, but the moment I saw Teacher Cai on the stairs, my knees almost buckled. It would seem that "juvenile influence" is rightly emphasized in many novels and films. I didn't want to stand facing the wall as punishment, so for the first time this year I wasn't late to an event.

This time, twenty female students and nine male students came. Ours was a special class. When I took my middle school exams for the first time, I got a combined 273 for all three subjects, with an average of 91 points out of 100 per subject. When I got home I told my parents with great joy and excitement that I had come in the top ten for the year. In the end it transpired that I was number forty-two. And from then on I began to self-destruct.

After nine years I had the sudden realization that the girls in our class were actually quite pretty after all. Perhaps it was because at the time I was completely focused on the class next door, Class Thirteen. I firmly believed back then that "a rabbit does not eat the grass next to its nest." In order to better control me, the teachers arranged for me to have a seat in the front row, so that "a good horse doesn't eat trodden grass." In retrospect this was meaningless: I'm not a rabbit or a horse, so what's it got to do with me how two random animals like to eat their grass?

The first event was a random drawing where if you were picked you had to go onstage and answer a question, or do a dare. I was never chosen, and the two MCs weren't too happy. They said I had to go up voluntarily to pick a question so I could embarrass myself. In the end the question I picked was: "You have the right to ask any ex-student any question and ask any ex-student to do anything."

After eating, the organizer suggested we play "Assassin" and took us out to a small pagoda in a park, where we could play sitting in a circle. For a moment I didn't get what we were playing. I'm normally as cold as my name, Han Han, implies,* but this was too chilly, even for me. Later, we decided to take the game to a karaoke parlor. I called my father to ask which of the local KTVs had the largest rooms. Our little town is so crappy that there aren't many proper KTV joints, and we were worried about being paired with KTV hosts. There

---

* Han Han's given name means "chill," and he blogs under the ID "twocold."

were twenty-nine of us, so they'd send twenty-nine ladies. Fifty-eight people playing "Assassin," and each of the ladies dressed the same, would make it really difficult. Our minds were put to rest when we entered the KTV joint: It was so crappy there weren't even any hosts.

As soon as we were about to start, my father called to say, "The ladies who sing with you are a 100 yuan each, so don't give them too much."

You could tell from that sum that consumer spending where I'm from is pretty low.

As I'm writing this, I suddenly thought: *My mother doesn't know how to get online, does she?*

I started flipping through my old blogs yesterday, beginning with the ones about car racing and dog raising in 2006, and ending with the recent ones, which were attempts to keep up the quality of the posts. Just two months ago I was still making the complaint that a good writer "slaughters" not only the elite but also the public. But I forgot about slaughtering myself. *Slaughter* is serious, not a term usually used freely on individuals. But sometimes there's more than one self. A person who does not "slaughter" the self is dangerous, because if he is then forced to kill himself a little, there's hell to pay, as there was in 1962 . . . and 1966 . . . and then there was the 70/30 split, and then the passing of the old guard.*

Once school starts, I'll head to my alma mater to begin lecturing. I think I've found a theme: In just seven months I'll be thirty years old. I'll tell those younger alumni that in these ten thousand–odd days I've made all kinds of mistakes and done things I've had to think about. I've never believed in

---

* The famine resulting from the Great Leap Forward forced Mao Zedong to make a self-criticism in 1962 and transfer some of his power, but he regained it with the launch of the Cultural Revolution in 1966. The official assessment is that, overall, his polices were 70 percent correct, 30 percent mistaken.

"success studies," so I detest the little television screens at airport bookshops where you can watch someone lecture about how he found success. Lots of things might not be transferable on the way to success, and besides, you can't pass on your own dumb luck to the audience, so looking at someone else's success is never helpful for your own. Still, hearing about someone else's failures might help you avoid failure yourself.

Flipping through my blog, I see that by 2011 I'd actually fallen into a malaise: I didn't know what to write, since I didn't want to repeat myself. How fortunate there are so many Chinese characters, or else I'd have given up long ago. I just flipped to 2008, and the events swim right before my eyes. There was a catastrophic blizzard, the Carrefour protests, the Sichuan earthquake, the Olympics, and the Sanlu milk scandal. And four years ago today, I wrote a post titled "This Generation," which many of you probably didn't notice. That was my first foray into writing serious essays.

Tonight my thoughts turn again to my generation. When I debuted I was the rebel, defying my seniors, and I left Shanghai for Beijing because I-can't-remember-who told me Beijing's the place to go if you're into culture. In those days there was no Fifth Ring Road and no bars in Houhai, my friends were at school, and adults spent their time messaging on ICQ or OICQ, and with no friends around I was as lonely as a toilet plunger. After turning on my computer, I couldn't write anything, because my accumulated life had already been used up. Four years later, having learned nothing except how to race, I returned to Shanghai and looked up the girl I'd pursued in high school. Not long after that, my classmates graduated from college and we broke up. Once, a friend asked me why newspapers were unreadable until after 2006. I told him that was the year our generation had graduated and entered the media world. I feel sorry that my friend didn't read newspapers in the mid-'90s, when the atmosphere and the papers were both good and, incidentally, an inspiration to me.

To describe a generation by ten years, as is often done, is narrow. I've always maintained that there is a clear demarcation between one generation and another. Is there a big difference between being born in 1989 or 1991? If I was born in the former year, I'd have increased chances of missing birthday messages if my birthday fell on a particularly sensitive day. Still, this hazy generation, which consists of people born at the end of the '70s, the '80s, and the start of the '90s, fills me with hope. They were born into an era of educational brainwashing, but they missed the era where people had each other seized and publicly criticized. Their textbooks brainwashed only the part of the brain that wouldn't remember, and the brainwashing material was so dry, it triggered rebellion. They felt cheated when the Internet and Western products came along, but they have no way to take revenge now, since they can't find out who cheated them. They struggle to make their way in society, and apart from scheming there is nothing else they can do. However, they work much harder because they missed the chance to profit from social upheaval. When I arrived in Beijing as a teen, I didn't bother to connect with my peers. I met a few older people, and even though they were nice, I now prefer friends from the same generation. I'm convinced we're supposed to bear witness to many things, even though everything we've gone through amounts to little more than dandruff.

I'm particularly looking forward to the social changes brought along by this generation once it amasses power. Power alters power. The government holds public power, but the human rights, the abilities, the social currency, and

even the powerlessness of individuals can coalesce into another power, which, given enough of it, can transform public
power. But transformation isn't the goal; restraint is. This is
what I lacked in my previous "My Generation" post. Some of
what we regard as progress is actually the advance of technology. In the end, only power is able to alter power, just like that
old saying: "The parts make the whole." So I wonder what
this generation will make up. Of course, although I think our
generation holds the most potential for a turnaround, it's not
as easy as the way Chinese people swipe a card and pick up
their merchandise. Four years on, this is my rewrite of the
subject. Although 2008's post was pretty good, I did the best I
could to smear the previous generations because I wanted to
ass-kiss ours. I even said, "The jerks and crooks of our generation haven't surfaced yet." So let me return to this topic once
every four years, and each time I'll dedicate it to my friends of
this generation.

INDEX

ABOUT THE AUTHOR

Han Han was born in 1982 to middle-class parents. After dropping out of high school, he wrote a novel, *Triple Door*, which became the most widely distributed literary work in China in the past twenty years. He has since become a star of the rally racing circuit, a film director, and an international celebrity. He lives in Shanghai.